Talking to Myself

Holding a community together in spirit while the pandemic was keeping us apart

Tom O'Neill

McGeary Media

Cover photo of the Avenue of Trees, Acklam Hall, Middlesbrough © Ryan Hall

We lived in a world
where we could plan
and organise everything,
and now we are
thrown into a world
where we do not know
what lies ahead

Contents

Introduction

On December 31st 2019, the World Health Organisation was informed of a cluster of cases of pneumonia of an unknown cause, initially detected in Wuhan, China. It was named as the Coronavirus (Covid-19) and it spread rapidly, potentially leading to severe respiratory problems and death.

The virus is thought to have reached the UK in late January 2020, and by mid-March, the government urged people to work from home and avoid public spaces. Schools were closed and the Catholic Church, too, announced that no public Mass should be celebrated.

On March 23rd, Prime Minister Boris Johnson announced the first "lockdown", with the public ordered to stay at home, except in certain specified circumstances. Places of worship were among the many buildings told to close their doors.

This is how this little book came about. As a means of keeping in touch with the parish community myself and keeping them in touch with each other, I decided to send out a little reflection—just a thought or two each week. This is a collection of those reflections.

It is not intended to be read as a book, as each reflection stands on its own, and is not connected to what goes before or what follows. So take them in the way they originated. Read the reflection, then put it away and think not only about what you, the reader, have read, but more importantly, what is going on inside yourself.

As a result, what are you thinking—what are you feeling? Here is where we find the quiet conversation between creator and creature. This is the *"pearl of great price"* Jesus spoke about. Here you locate Jesus and he finds you.

Each reflection in itself is only intended as a tool to help us get in touch with the flow of life that is inside all of us, something we all have in common—the life Jesus promised: *"I have come to give you life, life in abundance."*

These reflections will be helpful to people of all faiths and no faith because they speak to the heart. The aim is to help the reader get in touch with what is going on inside.

For although we live life on the outside, we carry it in the inside. And we understand life better and see it more clearly backwards, though we must live it forwards because that is the way life comes to us. Here is where we all find ourselves in this busy, pressurised world that God loved so much he sent his only son to save.

Let us enter the two common grounds we all share: the human heart and the world we live in. They speak to the heart and to this all too often battered and broken, yet beautiful world.

I have been to dozens of
Masses of the Lord's Supper
and none have ever taken me
to this depth of feeling

Talking to Myself

Now that we are all tucked away in self-isolation, I have felt the urge to reach out and contact the living. I have a habit of talking to myself from time to time and I thought if I shared some of my words with you then I wouldn't feel so bad about this unusual behaviour of mine.

Yesterday morning was our last public Mass and it had a strange feeling of grief and sadness about it. There was a sense of loss and loneliness amid the gathering. We acknowledged it would be our last Mass for some time and that was the pain we were all carrying. We lived in a world where we could plan and organise everything, and now we are thrown into a world where we do not know what lies ahead.

The thought struck me that I have been to dozens of Masses of the Lord's Last Supper on Holy Thursday and none have ever taken me to this depth of feeling. I knew something more now of how the apostles would have felt, the anxiety and fear of what was to come. We were having our own Holy Thursday and we knew it. We could feel it in a very real way. The Lord seemed to say something quite clear to us all:

'Look around you and see the divisions among you—cultural, national and global. You can no longer go on putting your own group or country first. You are all one family and like every family you must live together as one, taking special care to look after the weaker members.'

We need to be concerned about the divisions both within our society and on an international level. We need to see the frictions of trade and other tensions that have developed over recent years. This can be an opportunity for a new beginning where we gather as one global village which, as we can see on our TV screens every day, is what we are.

What we have in common is far greater than the differences that set us apart. We have a common humanity and we are all made for Eternity—good and bad alike. And the line between good and bad is not outside of us. Both exist within every human heart. The good news is that all of us together make up the Body of Christ. So for the sake of Christ, it is important that we all get together and learn to live as one.

Lazarus

I not only talk to myself but also from time to time do a little thinking out loud. So I'd like to take you on one of these trips with me. The thought occurred to me when I looked at the gospel last Sunday (Jesus gives sight to the blind man) and again this Sunday (Jesus raises Lazarus from the grave), *'What is he trying to teach the apostles?'*

It is important to remember that everything Jesus says and does is always with the intention of teaching. He never works a miracle of any kind for the sake of sensationalism. In fact, sometimes after a miracle he specifically instructs the apostles not to tell anybody about it. In giving sight to the blind man, Jesus is teaching the apostles (and us) that in some way all of humankind is blind to the bigger picture. We don't seem able to see all that is around us. He wants to open our hearts and minds as well as our eyes to see more clearly and more deeply what is before us, around us and indeed what is within us.

He is teaching that the blind man is you and me and all of humankind. In the same way as he heals the blind man, he wants to open my eyes and heart and mind so I can blossom into the full version of myself. It is because there is so much more available that he wants us all to have that life in abundance.

Now on to Lazarus. It is important to note that Jesus never attended a funeral in the gospels and on the occasions when he came across a funeral, he raised the dead person to life and gave them back to their family. His message is that God is stronger than death. He wants to show his apostles that death (the great enemy) does not have the last word. He has destroyed death forever and restored life. Yes, one day it will capture each of us, but the moment it does, God steps in and rescues us from death. That is why it is never accurate to say, 'God has taken my loved one.' No. God will never do that to me. God does what Jesus is doing and just as Jesus wept at the grave of Lazarus, so, too, God weeps at every graveside. Death has taken my loved one but God has rescued them from death and one day God will give my loved one back to me.

This is the God that Jesus wants to open us up to and wipe from our eyes the cataracts that cause us to see God in any other way. This is the kind of God we can all love, the one we want on our side. It is the God I want to worship and the God I want to be close to every day, especially when I lose someone I love.

God did not bring about the death of Lazarus but as he rescued him from death, he used it as an opportunity to teach. Neither did he bring about the pandemic. So as he rescues us from our present situation, could he use this in the same way as an opportunity to teach us something about ourselves—if our minds and hearts and eyes are open to it?

Holy Week

I had hoped to have a parish Reconciliation Service this week but as somebody once said, 'Life is what happens to you while you are busy making other plans!'

Talking about reconciliation reminds me of a story about my mother. She lived to the ripe old age of 100 and she drove her car to ninety (ninety years old that is, not miles per hour!). Every morning she would pick up her friend Sophie and drive her to Mass. One morning, she noticed Sophie did not receive Holy Communion but she didn't say anything. The next day, as Sophie got out of the car, she muttered:

'I'm going into Mass again—and again I can't receive.'

'And why can you not receive?' asked my mother.

'Because I swore,' answered Sophie.

'What do you mean, you swore?'

'Well, I got home the other day from a visit to my neighbour, put my hand in my pocket for the key and said to myself, "Jesus! I've left my key at the neighbour's house."'

'That wasn't swearing at all,' said my mother. 'That was a prayer.'

'So can I go to Holy Communion then?'

'Of course you can!'

Later, as she recounted the story to me, my mother declared, *'I absolved her straight away. Wasn't I right?'*

We are entering Holy Week, the great reconciliation event that flows through all of creation. The whole week must be seen as one event, and most important of all, Holy Week is an inside job and can only be properly understood in this way. By that I mean it is what is going on inside of Jesus that saves, not the suffering. If we look only on the externals—the cruelty and suffering—then we miss the point. It is the love he has for us that drives him through all that suffering. It is something like the mother who rushes into the burning building to rescue her child. It is her love for her child that drives her into the building. The bond between the mother and child is stronger than the fire. And it is the bond between Jesus and us that drives him through.

This is why I think the Mel Gibson film *The Passion of Christ* is so far off the mark. It is all about the terrible torture of the Passion. Yes, crucifixion is brutal and barbaric, but that is not where the emphasis should lie. What does need to be emphasised, over and over again, is that Jesus loves us so much he will go through all of this and anything else that may come his way for no other reason than to show us that nothing will separate us from him—just as nothing is going to stop that mother rushing into the burning building to rescue her child.

So when we come to Holy Week with that understanding, we can see it from the inside out. It is only then that we begin to catch an awareness of what is going on. That love of Christ is constantly pouring into you and me and I need to open my heart so his love can flow into me and out through me. And this is not theory or some academic exercise. This is reality. It is going on now. As we are loved, so we love. As we are forgiven, so we forgive. As we receive mercy, so we show mercy. As our lives are transformed, so we will transform others. Now, although all of this love flowing from Jesus is free and available, accepting it is very costly. It is nothing less than letting Christ live in me. How much I have grasped Holy Week is not how well I can talk about it, but how much of his life is flowing through me. It is not about me getting through Holy Week, it is about Holy Week getting through me. Returning to my good mother, of course, we all know she could not really absolve her friend. Or could she? And did she?

Resurrection

In the past two weeks we have had two resurrection stories: Lazarus and Jesus. Two very different resurrections, and it is important for us to note the distinction.

The resurrection of Lazarus shows us that God is stronger than death and that death does not have the last word. It also prepares us for the Resurrection of Jesus, a much fuller and larger resurrection. The first only applies to Lazarus, his family and community, the people of his time and place. The Resurrection of Jesus has consequences for the whole of humanity and indeed for the whole of creation. When Jesus raised Lazarus, he brought him back again to this same world he had left when he died. He would be the same Lazarus, with his family and friends. He would continue with the same limitations we all experience in life. He would succeed and fail again, get sick and recover. He would grow old and eventually die again.

But Jesus went right through death and came out the other side to a radically new and larger life—life without limitation. Now he could be everywhere and anywhere and he could let himself be seen when he chose. He was seen by Mary Magdalene in the garden, by the apostles locked away in fear in the upper room, by two of his disciples on a country road on the way to Emmaus, and he came walking on the water to his disillusioned apostles who had returned to their fishing. He is with us always and everywhere now in this new and limitless life.

That is only the beginning of the Good News of Easter. The next part is even better. It means that all our loved ones who have gone ahead of us have been taken right through death in the same way as Jesus and are living that limitless life with him, too. So when Jesus says, *'I will not leave you; I am with you always,'* our loved ones are saying the same to us. This is why we experience that they have left us and yet are still with us. They are gone and yet not gone, absent from our lives and yet truly present. We cannot explain it, nor do we need to. It is our experience and we know it to be true.

Every time I go home to Ireland, I find myself drawn to the village graveyard. Now I know, as every Christian knows, that every grave is an empty grave. I am not going to see dead people because they are not here. This is the Good News because of the first Easter Sunday. They are with Christ in his new life and so they are with me everywhere, as is Christ. This great army of lovely people are surrounding me and supporting me as I go about my daily tasks. The names and dates on the headstones serve as a kind of roll call—a reminder of those who are present with me all the time. It is tangible and there is a peace about this place. For a few moments I can be present to them, call them by name and in many cases, enjoy a trip down Memory Lane.

The graveyard is a village in itself on the outskirts of the village, and maybe it's more than geographical. It says something deeply personal. All these ones who were part of my growing up, helped shape who I am, moulded my character and passed on the faith that inspires me today are still very much with me, at my shoulder and supporting me on my journey. Yes, Resurrection is for real. It is part of our lives now and what we experience now does not unravel at death. Alleluia!

This Easter, may he rise again in a new way among you, your families and all those you love.

The Empty Tomb in Church

Walking into the church on Easter Monday morning, I was hit by the bare Lenten sanctuary. I stood and stared for a while before I turned round and fixed my gaze on the empty pews. And then it all began. As I walked up and down the church, I was overcome with feelings of both gratitude and humility, knowing I am called to minister to all you lovely people of God. The seed of God is there in you and it is my privilege to water and nurture it—to bring it to full bloom. You have all been baptised and anointed in the priesthood of Christ so this glorious, resurrected life can be taken out into every home, every family, every parish and every place of work. Now my responsibility is to get this life flowing out from you people and this community. Your responsibility is to respond to that call so that the Risen Christ is 'going out ahead of us into Galilee'. And Galilee for Christ is where each one of us lives and works and that is where he wants to be.

Now we do not need to be concerned about *understanding* how this can be so. No. It is about *awareness*. Am I aware that Christ is alive and living in me *now, today*? It might be a lovely prayer in the evening as I rest a while with Jesus and allow myself to be interviewed by him. How do I think I fared today? Did I allow myself to be led by him, let him live in me and have his way in me? And I can ask him how he felt today, living in me? Did he feel free and that he could be himself in me, or did he feel tied down as if he were still in the tomb? The priesthood of our baptism is far superior to the ministerial priesthood. It is the eternal life of the Risen Christ living in us as opposed to a function or a role within the community of the baptised. So if I tend to these seeds of baptism in this community they will bud and blossom and they, in turn, will ordain me, again and again, as they have done so many times in the past. We will all burst into bloom together and be the real sign of the Risen Christ. I left the church excited and amazed, much like Mary Magdalene went from the empty tomb after meeting her Risen Lord. And like her, being a slow learner it took me a little while to realise what was going on around me. I did not recognise him at first and then slowly it began to dawn on me that Christ was with me and telling me that he is now risen and living in you people and wherever you are now, that is where I would find him. And just as he sent Mary to tell the apostles, he was saying to me, *'Go now and tell them the Good News that I have risen from the dead and that I am now living in them. From now on, wherever they go, I will go and wherever they live, I will live.'*

What dignity. And it is yours and mine—a free gift from our Risen Lord. Alleluia!

It is connection
without physical,
tangible presence-
we are bonded together
by missing each other

Spiritual Communion

What do we mean when we talk about receiving Communion spiritually? The first thing we have to say is that it's not just some 'churchy thing' we do at Mass. No. It is much more than that. We are *all* experts in what it means because we have been living it and feeling it since lockdown began. It is a process that's going on in our lives. We live in it just like fish in the ocean and are carried along with its ebb and flow every day. It is connection without physical, tangible presence. What binds us together now is the very pain of missing each other. It is the pain of separation, deprivation and loss. It is a longing for a part of me to be returned to myself. It means being connected with family, friends and carers now by pain and ache. We are bonded together by missing each other and all that goes with those missing feelings.

It also raises up memories that are both a blessing and a curse at the same time—memories of when we could be together and now we can't.

This pull at the heartstrings is the Communion, the raw aching feeling that connects us now. Isn't it strange that the very pain that ties us together is our comfort now? That seems such a paradox and yet we know it to be true. These are the invisible strings that we know to be so very real. This is Spiritual Communion. We are together personally yet without seeing, hearing or touching. We are present and aware of each other in a different and new way. It could be said we are communicating now from the inside out.

The same is true for the sacraments. If I am deprived of the sacraments of the Church, this pain of separation will be experienced in my soul, my person, my inside. This is a real part of me that has been separated and cut away from myself and I will ache until it is returned. All too often we take what we have for granted. We tell ourselves it is the norm but it isn't. Everything is pure gift, grace and blessing. It does us no harm now and again for these 'normal' things to be taken from us for a while and then returned to let us know how much they had become part of us. I am not the full me without my 'inside'. This is communion with my loved ones, communion with my soul and communion with my God. In short, this is me fully human, fully alive.

Our most intense experience of Spiritual Communion is the pain of brokenness and loss when someone we love dies. It is the mental blank and the numbness of heart. Everything that was my world is now gone and I am no longer the 'me' that was. I am but a shell. Even my energy has left me. When we lose somebody, it can feel as though they have taken with them the best of who we are. However, with the passage of time a healing takes place and it seems as if the spirit of my loved ones slowly come back to me, and so what were painful memories also become a comforting presence. And it is not so much brokenness and pain that fills my heart; instead it is now a comfortable companionship. Am I already experiencing death and resurrection? Yes, all these mysteries are going on in us and now we have the time to ponder them.

So when we receive Holy Communion these days without receiving at all, we are touching and making contact with all these areas of our lives. It connects us with our lived experience.

A Further Reflection on Spiritual Communion

Now that we are all living our Spiritual Communion and know what it feels like, we are in a better position to reflect on the experience. How do our brothers and sisters, sons and daughters feel when they find themselves in a loving relationship after having come through the trauma of a previous marriage breakdown, only to be told they can no longer take part fully in the Eucharist? For whatever reason, it would appear that the people of God have not been as generous and understanding as the God revealed to us by Jesus Christ.

Sure enough they have made a mistake, fallen short, been sinned against or were dealt a bad hand. This is true for all of us in various situations in our lives. The human condition is such that we all fail, but we can get up, dust ourselves down, forgive and begin again. Why is marriage breakdown the one occasion where we are not allowed to get up and make a new start?

If we are to be consistent with the Gospel, there would be no such thing as Spiritual Communion for anybody apart from something like a pandemic, when we are all barred from our churches and it is the only option. But even if there were, who should be the ones to go without? What mother would prepare the Sunday roast for her family and refuse to allow one of her children to join in the meal? *'Does a mother forget...the child of her womb?' (Isaiah 49:15) '...who would hand his son a stone when he asked for bread?' (Matt 7:9)*

Maybe we would have a better experience of community if we all fasted from Communion in solidarity with our brother or sister until we can find a way for everyone to be together at the table of the Lord. It would increase our urgency to find a way forward. And perhaps the process of fasting may make the whole community hungry for Holy Communion. What a lovely thing that would be—a parish community hungry for the Eucharist!

Another question worth asking ourselves is from where do we get our Eucharistic values? Are we bringing in our guidelines from the world outside and imposing them on the Eucharist? Those who succeed are rewarded and get the prize. There is nothing for the loser. The rich get richer and the poor get poorer. Those who fail are the casualties. Instead, we could draw out from the Eucharist the values we find in the teaching and practice of Christ. He sits at table with all kinds of waifs and strays, the broken and wounded, the sinners and outcasts. This is the Eucharist that Christ welcomes us all to, where everyone is included and there are no outsiders. It is the Field Hospital Church that Pope Francis speaks about so often.

If the Eucharist does not pick up the sinner, the poor, the blind, the broken, then where can we turn? It was a motley crew that sat around Our Lord's table the night before he died! Peter dipped in and so did Judas. Yes, the Eucharist is medicine for the sick and the weak. It is not a prize for the successful.

A Reflection on the Mass We are Missing So Much

We would probably all do ourselves a favour—people and priests—if we used this time when the Mass has been taken from us to reflect on what we were doing at the Mass we are missing so much.

Through the sacrament of baptism, we have all been ordained as priests and so it falls to every one of us to offer the priestly prayer of Christ at Mass. The Mass *is* Christ praying to his Father for the whole world and we all join our voices with his as we are ordained to do. The theologian Ronald Rolheiser OMI suggests that when we offer this priestly prayer, we do so *'as a microcosm of the earth itself, to give it voice,'* asking God to see in our sincerity, our hypocrisy, our generosity and our selfishness the world's sincerity, hypocrisy, generosity and selfishness. He goes on to hold up in prayer all the joy, suffering, achievements and failures of the world, the powerful, the rich, the young and the healthy as well as *'those who are weak, feeble, aged, crushed, sick, dying and victimised'*, before concluding with the words:

'I offer you both the wonders and the pains of this world, your world.'[1]

This is why my presence at Mass is *so* important, because I am bringing so much of the world with me. I am not there as a spectator but as a vital participant, fulfilling my priestly duty and privilege received at my baptism. Everyone at Mass brings so much of the world with them as members of Christ's body; it means Christ is more present because we are there. What a glorious calling and responsibility, to join with Christ in holding up the world and praying for it! Here we have the distinction between liturgical prayer and private prayer. The former is concerned with Christ's intentions and not with my own. The latter is personal and will be concerned with my own intentions. This is your weekly invitation, and mine: to join Christ in his prayer to his Father for the world—the Mass.

---

1. From the article *Priestly Prayer—Prayer for the World,* March 16th 2003. Reprinted with permission.

A Further Reflection on the Mass

We began our last reflection in awe and wonder at the company we joined. Following on from this, the conversation begins between God and us in the Liturgy of the Word. Note the movement: God speaks to us through the first reading. We respond through the responsorial psalm. Jesus speaks through the Gospel and we respond again, this time with ourselves.

We offer bread, wine and the collection plate. These are deeply symbolic because they carry all that we are. Bread is the symbol of our sin and our goodness. We have too much of it for ourselves, while the poorer countries go hungry. And at the same time, it symbolises our generosity in sharing with those in need. Wine is the bottle that can bring so much misery and brokenness but it can also be the bonding of unity, joy and celebration. The collection plate symbolises our whole working week, now offered; we give ourselves to God just as we are, good and bad.

Now Christ takes these gifts from us and he prays over them in the Eucharistic Prayer that this bread and wine will become his Body and Blood—the Consecration. Next, he prays over us that we may be transformed into 'one body, one Spirit in Christ'—and we become his body. But he does not leave us to our own devices. He comes in Holy Communion to assist us in this glorious privilege. In this way he can continue to live in our bodies, in the places where we live and work, in our pain and our joy.

Finally, he sends us out transformed, transfigured and nourished. All he requires now is our cooperation. He will be living in the world this week, in us and in everything that is going on in your life and mine. Just like the football manager, Jesus is saying as we leave the church, 'Now you are crossing the white line onto the pitch of my world, so go out there, enjoy yourselves and give me your very best performance, as I know you can!' his effectiveness in the world is in our hands. That is the faith he has in each one of us. So when we hear, *'The Mass is ended. Go in peace,'* it is only the church part, the preparation that is ended. In a real sense we should hear, 'The Mass has now *begun*. Go in peace.'

The elements of the universe
are all caught up
in the great events
of Christ's life:
His birth, Crucifixion,
Resurrection,
Ascension and Pentecost

Ascension Thursday

Our faith only makes sense at the point at which we can see it unfolding in front of us, when we become aware that we are part of something much greater than ourselves, when we can feel it going on in us and see it taking place all around us. Then, and only then, will our faith catch fire with voltage and energy. Faith is not to be confused with doctrine. It is about waking up—and there are different stages of being awake. It is always about *life* that is going on now in you and in me and in all of creation. It is seeing and recognising what is before our eyes. Bearing this in mind, let us look at Ascension and reflect on what it means.

Christ has done something for us by his death and Resurrection and we will never be the same again. It means we are now living the resurrected life of Christ. We are all taken up into a new state—a new level. So it is more accurate to say, 'We have all been taken up' rather than 'Christ was taken up'—because Christ does not leave us. He does not go anywhere on his own. We are always with him. So now he has brought us into the same bond and relationship with our Heavenly Father as he himself has. *'Many people longed to … hear what you hear and did not hear it.' (Matthew 13:17)* This is what Ascension means. It is our ascension just as much as Christ's.

Parents are looking at this every day in their children. We know it in ourselves as we grow in new awareness and wisdom. We see it in great and small acts of generosity and heroism all around us. We see it in the streets as workers do repairs and people improve their homes and gardens. Our flower beds are bursting out with colour and fragrance. Fields are filling up with crops. Seed is constantly rising to bud, blossom and fruit.

Ascension is a process that is going on in all of creation and we are part of that process. It is not something we *believe* in any more than oxygen is something we believe in. It is much more than that. It is the very life that flows through us, and through everything that lives. In the words of the Jesuit priest poet Gerard Manley Hopkins, *'The world is charged with the grandeur of God.'*[1]

---

1. The first line of the poem, *God's Grandeur* (1877)

The Resurrection Of Christ

And How We Experience it in Our Lives

Christ's Resurrection is much more than the individual Resurrection of Jesus himself. It is corporate and the whole of creation is involved—the sun, the moon and the stars in the sky, the mountains and hills, the rivers and oceans and all that live in them. Every living thing is affected by this glorious event. And so humankind, on behalf of all creation, will come together and give praise to God for what he has done. It began with the Incarnation and comes to climax with the Resurrection.

This is why you will find all the elements of the universe are caught up in the great events of Christ's life: his birth, Crucifixion, Resurrection, Ascension and Pentecost. A star led the wise men to the newborn infant; darkness covered the whole land at the Crucifixion; there was a violent earthquake at the Resurrection, the rush of a mighty wind at Pentecost and at the Ascension, Jesus was taken up in a cloud. The whole of creation is affected. Nothing will ever be the same again. This life is going on all around us and we are part of it.

St Paul is full of exuberance at the awareness of this and his letters reflect it. He tells us we have gone into the grave with Christ and we have risen with him *(Romans 6:8)* so that the life we have now is the Risen Life of Christ. This is true for you and me and the whole of humanity. This is the great gift Christ has given to each of us.

This life is in us and we may experience it as a kind of restlessness or frustration. I always want more for myself and my family, for my business, my home and so on. But no matter what I achieve or accumulate, I am never fulfilled completely. That is because I am wired for something which is bigger than I am. My reach will always outstretch my grasp, and I will never be fully satisfied. I am made for more. This is not greed, although that is something that could materialise if I do not recognise the source of this drive within me, because then I will go to the wrong location to find nourishment for this hunger within me. I may find myself accumulating, collecting money, property and honours, and being caught up in all kinds of achievements to satisfy my restlessness.

The danger is that I may become aggressive, pushing my way forward and sacrificing people, events and communities to reach my goals. This is not uncommon in the world we live in today. Goals are a wonderful thing and God-given, in the correct place. But when they drive me to fulfil my selfish and misguided ambition, then I am on a road to destruction. This is why it is important to locate the source of my restlessness and to identify it for what it is—the Resurrected Christ-life in me. St Augustine put it very well: *'Lord you have made us for yourself and our hearts are restless until they rest in you'*[1]. Once I discover this and acknowledge it, I will begin to be at peace and on the road to living a more fulfilled life for myself and those around me.

---

1. From *Confessions* (St Augustine of Hippo, written between AD 397 and 400)

Pentecost

Good religion will lead us to God. Bad religion will shield us from God. Pentecost is a case in point. This feast is not to be understood as the Holy Spirit coming down on the Apostles and into our world for the first time. The very first action of the Holy Spirit was the dawn of creation over thirteen billion years ago. And the Creator Spirit has been pouring into and through every molecule of creation ever since. Pentecost is an acknowledgment of this and draws our attention to the workings of the Spirit all around us. The whole of creation is charged with this life. As we become aware of the Spirit in creation, we will become aware of the Spirit in ourselves. This will give us a new vision and we will stop pushing God back into our churches and into heaven, because we will see him *now* where he is—everywhere we look, in all creation.

This is not to be confused with pantheism, which claims that the material world *is* God and all the forces of the universe together *are* God.

St Paul is quite clear in his distinct teaching that the Spirit comes to us through creation and that indeed *'the whole of creation is groaning in one great act of giving birth'* to a new heaven and a new earth *(Romans 8:22).* The planet we live on is a sacred sanctuary filled with the presence of the Spirit. Pope Francis spells this out for us time and time again in his teachings.

So where do we look to find the Spirit at work in creation? The garden is always a good place to start, where all kinds of things are going on silently, all filled with new life. See the colours, smell the freshness, touch the flowers, listen to the birds singing their praises. All around us we see ties of love and affection: husbands and wives; lovers and loved ones; parents and children; brothers and sisters; friends and neighbours. And this bonding is the Spirit grafting us together as one. The Spirit creates new life—human, animal, plant and even mineral.

Because we find God's Spirit in all creation, we want to come together in church to thank him and there we meet him again in the Eucharist. Note the work of the Spirit here: *'Send your Spirit on these gifts...'* (bread and wine) and again after the consecration, *'Send your Spirit on us so that we may become one body, one Spirit...'* The challenge here is, do I leave myself open to be changed as the bread and wine are changed? Am I leaving Mass more at one with my loved ones, my family and friends, those around me and at work? This is the work of the Spirit at Mass. It is quiet, gentle and secret, something that goes on all the time, as silently as the falling blossom.

The Spirit is in failure, too, and Jesus saw plenty of that. He wept over Jerusalem and longed to gather the people as a hen gathers her chicks, but they wouldn't listen. The apostles didn't understand. Peter denied him, Judas betrayed him and they all deserted him as it ended with crucifixion and failure. Yes, we see the Spirit of God in failure and defeat, often more powerfully than anywhere else. In suffering and illness, we see fortitude; in the breakup of a relationship, we see strength to carry on; a single parent, having been abandoned, shows sheer heroism bringing up the children alone, and how often we see the extended family bond there to support. The Spirit is at work all around us, but we need eyes that see much deeper than the surface.

Of course, all failures culminating on Calvary are short term. Easter Sunday makes them part of the great success story—yours and mine included. Because we are all united with Christ by the Holy Spirit, his victory and success are our victory and success too. All of this we celebrate on Pentecost Sunday.

How Did Three Persons in One God Come About?

This is a simple view of our ancestors' knowledge and experience of their God. Next week, we can have a reflection on our own personal faith story—our little mini tradition of whatever number of years we have lived—and see how it fits into our ancestors' story. Tradition is as important as memory. What memory is for the person, tradition is for the community. So how have you experienced your God—Father, Son and Spirit?

When we look back in hindsight we can see more clearly, even if we don't understand it. This is what our ancestors did and passed down to us. When they first knew God he revealed himself in the elements—wind, cloud, thunder, storms. This is how he spoke to them. He helped them through many difficulties and made a covenant with them: he would be their God and they would be his people. But although he was a wonderful support and comfort to them, he was always at a distance and they could never get close to him or meet him face to face.

Then one of their own called Jesus, who grew up among them, showed himself to be great and wonderful in every way. He taught them and made a deep impression on everyone. He worked many miracles and wonders. But he claimed to be God, saying: 'Whoever has seen me has seen the Father' (John 14:9). He even went further and said: 'I and the Father are one' (John 10:30).

This was a step too far because the people knew there was only one God and he had made it clear to them that there was no other God but himself. So they crucified him and he was buried. But that wasn't the end of him. He rose again from the dead. All this was a real experience for them, as clear as night follows day.

Now this risen one told them he would go away but would be with them in a different way. He would send his Spirit and in this way he would be with them from inside each one. And then it happened, and they knew they were different—no longer frightened. They had a new courage and were changed completely and nothing was more real. It was like being born again. They went out to the whole of the known world to tell the Good News to everyone.

When our people look back over their story they can only tell us what happened to them and how they have experienced their God. He is only one God and he made that clear—yet they experienced him in three very different ways, over many centuries, generation after generation. And they have simply told us of their experience of this God who has come to them in this mysterious way:

1. He is a loving, caring father
2. He is a constant companion
3. He is a powerful life inside of them.

And all of this at the same time! They can't explain it and that is not important to them. What is important for them is to pass on to us how they have known and experienced God, so that we can link our experience with theirs and so find support and companionship in our common faith journey with our God. This is their story in a nutshell. We call it tradition—our tradition.

The Blessed Trinity

Our Experience

How many persons have you experienced in God and in yourself? Last week we reflected on how our ancestors experienced God in their lives and their history, three very different experiences of the one God—Father, Son and Spirit. With that as a background, we can now reflect on how we experience the Father, Son and Spirit in our lives and in our history.

What has been our early experience? What did our parents and grandparents tell us? Where did they find God? They found him in the silent Mass, the Latin, the mystery, the Rosary, devotions, processions and the parish community. The God of our fathers, the Faith of Our Fathers (and mothers, more often) will be our first experience of God. What kind of God did our parents, teachers and priests pass on to us? Are our memories of home strict and duty-bound or loving and delightful—with the usual fights, or maybe a mixture of both? What were we taught in school and what was the Church saying about God? This will have had a large influence on our image of God the Father.

What about our experience of Jesus? This will be more personal and will be different for each one of us. It is no longer what others say about God; what is important now is what is going on between Jesus and me. I ask myself now, *where have I felt closest to Jesus?* It may be at Mass, Holy Communion, as a parent, a child, a partner, in friendship, in sickness, in bereavement, in nature, in music, in art, in prayer. The list goes on because there are as many ways to connect with Jesus as there are people. There will be times when I am more aware of him and feel him closer than at others.

And where do we find the Holy Spirit—the Spirit that ties us to one another with bonds of love and affection? We can see close families in open and welcoming homes, friends laughing together as they pass on the street, children delighting in each other's company as they play. The Spirit that gives courage can be seen in the elderly, sick lady as she lies so tranquil in her bed. The Spirit will always stretch us out, so the way we relate to God will always evolve and grow. We will find that the way we pray is not the way we used to. Our faith is not like it once was. In fact sometimes we may begin to fear that we are losing our faith, that we had more faith when we were younger. This is because the Spirit is at work in us, giving us a larger capacity for a fuller and more mature faith for this stage of our lives. In the words of the psalm, we can feel *'like a dry, weary land without water' (Psalm 63).* This is constantly changing and growing when the Spirit is at work in us.

We won't ever understand this mystery, any more than we understand the mystery of life. But like all mysteries, we experience something of it every day.

Never forget,
you are the Church
at home with your family

There is No Need to Be Afraid

We all long for the day when we can be together again to celebrate the Eucharist. That day will come in the Lord's good time. In the meantime, there is a little thought I would like to share with you.

You will be familiar with the picture of Jesus with the lantern in one hand and knocking at the door with the other to get into our hearts. The quote that goes with it is: *'Behold I stand at the door and knock' (Rev 3:20)*. A few days before he was elected, Pope Francis said to his then fellow cardinals, 'I have the impression that Jesus was locked inside the Church and that he was knocking because he wanted to get out!' It makes a lot of sense because *'God loved the world so much that he sent his only son to save it' (John 3:16)*.

Right now, this lovely world is sick, suffering and wounded in so many ways and God is out in the midst of it in you and me. It is where he wants to be at this time. And if we need any reassurance, he tells us three times in the Gospel this Sunday, *'There is no need to be afraid.'*

We Are the Church

(On June 11th 2020, the government announced that churches could open but only for private prayer and under strict conditions)

I am so grateful to those of you who have offered to help get the church ready to open for prayer but I think we all understand that now is not the right time. There is a great deal to organise and most of our volunteers are in the vulnerable category, while others have to return to work or have families to look after.

All of this makes me think of Pope Francis' words when he tells us that families are the 'domestic Church'. During these strange times, I have come to realise more than ever before that the *real* Church is in our homes.

It was from our families that we learnt everything about faith. That seed was planted in us when we were very young and it is our grandparents, our parents and families who have nurtured that faith in us. In the same way, they taught us to know Jesus. It was from our mothers' knees that we first learnt how to pray and it was in the family that we learnt to love, to care and to forgive—to be in communion with one another.

Today, Jesus grows in you and in your children and in the same way that our grandparents, parents and families gave us their faith and taught us to know Jesus, so we can pass this on to our children. The family is where our faith can continue to grow and the place where Jesus is living.

Pope Francis talks a lot about grandparents and I can understand why, because I am continually inspired when I see them with their grandchildren, coming and going from school. Parents are busy working and often have other things going on but grandparents have the freedom to enjoy their grandchildren and in doing so, they are passing on their wisdom and the faith of the Church.

Never forget, you are the Church at home with your family. In fact, you are never more the Church than when you are at home with your family. And while we all look forward to celebrating the Eucharist again together, we continue to live in our little domestic Church, at the same time joining our Mass and Spiritual Communion, as we do now.

Holy Family of Nazareth, grant that our families, too, may be places of communion and prayer, authentic schools of the Gospel, and small domestic Churches (Pope Francis).

Prayer

(Although churches had been permitted to open for private prayer since June 15th, there was a series of legal requirements which took time to plan and implement)

Now that churches are beginning to open for private prayer, I think it is worth a reflection. While it is good to pray in church, we can also pray wherever we happen to find ourselves. But we must find a way to understand what we mean by prayer. Otherwise, we will drift through life and never really pray, which will put all kinds of limitations on our quality of life.

'Can I have a beer when I am praying?' the student asked his master.

'Oh no,' replied the master, *'that would be disrespectful.'*

'Can I pray when I am having a beer?' he asked.

'Oh yes, you can pray anywhere and at any time.'

It is a great pity some of us older folks were never shown how to pray but thank God that has changed and one of my delights now is to be in the school classroom when the little ones are being guided through a meditation. They take to it like ducks to water. We can all pray naturally if we have someone to show us the way.

Prayer is not something we do for God. It is something God does in us and through us. God does not work in fits and starts, but *all* the time. He is working and living in you, day and night, in everything you do and in all that you are. A key ingredient to a healthy prayer life is a growing awareness of this. Christ goes on living his Paschal Mystery now in your life and in mine. That is what we mean by 'Incarnation'. We experience this in any kind of suffering and little deaths and resurrections in our lives. Every breath you take is *his* breath in you and through *your* lungs.

We have been taught that prayer is 'saying prayers' and that is the first step for a child. Sadly, this is where most of us were dropped off. And our minds are as capable of running away with us as our legs. It is this that sabotages our prayer life and our relationship with God and why we don't pray as often as we might wish. This isn't anyone's fault; it is simply that nobody guided us through the next step and the next step again.

In our relationship with God, we need knowledge that is good and wholesome. Take the phrase: *'The Lord takes delight in his people' (Psalm 194:4).* Let those words sink in. He takes delight in *you.* Now take a little time out, relax in a comfortable chair, maybe with a glass of wine. Recall your day, the situations you were in and the people you met. Now without the temptation to judge and condemn yourself, just let it play and see how Christ lived in you today. This is what actually happened because the Incarnation is our faith just as the Paschal Mystery is our faith.

Christ is not only living *in* you but he is living *as* you now. Unless we are aware of this, we won't even want to pause and spend time with him.

This is prayer for the adult. And to miss out on it is tragic because it is the connection to a better, far richer quality of life we could not have even imagined. We will be more at peace with ourselves. We will begin to overflow with gratitude and the increase in our intimacy will make us hungry for more prayer like this. We become more aware of God in our lives, in the joy and the laughter, the mess and the mud, everything that makes up our day. Prayer is the oxygen of the Christian life, so make sure you have a daily supply.

Living on the Surface

Last week we reflected on the importance of resting for a while with God and enjoying his presence. We don't need to say anything—just be aware of him looking at us and loving us. I read somewhere the other day that many people do not believe in God anymore. And this is true not only of folk who claim to be atheists but also those who have been believers until recently, many of whom were churchgoers. What is concerning about this is that if people don't believe in *something* then they will believe in *anything*. The advertising industry is aware of this and that's why a fortune is spent on it—because it succeeds in encouraging people to live on the surface!

Why is this so? It is because we have inherited a world that not only does our thinking for us but also our seeing—how far we see and how deeply we see. We see the surface of things and of people too, so we have to constantly work hard to ensure this does not affect our relationships. While we remain on the surface, we will struggle to find God because God is the *centre* of everything.

This world has an elaborate and persuasive plan for us all, so there is no need for us to think or reflect for ourselves. The world will do it for us. The supermarkets and stores provide the options. The television tells us what to choose. The tabloids and magazines provide us with guidance. Bingo and clubs are food for some, while restaurants and shows are for others; sport in its thousand forms helps us release our energy; travel appeals to our inner restlessness and when we need to rest there is no shortage of holiday destinations available. So all our wants and needs are provided for—on the surface.

But the surface is not where we meet God because God is at the centre of everything and everyone. He is at the centre of the universe, the earth, the oceans, the skies, the stars. He is at the centre of every event, every action and all energy. He is at the centre of you and the centre of me.

So hopefully the lockdowns have not been all bad if they have given us time to reflect and discover our God in the deeper part of ourselves and our families. And as we look forward to returning to normal, our churches and our families, we will be different. Our faith will have grown and the way we pray may not be the same. There may have been times when we were afraid we were losing our faith, but all the time it was God working in us and giving us an even greater capacity for him and a new awareness of him in our lives. And because we have found him in a new way in our deepest selves, we can easily locate him everywhere now.

Returning

Coming Home to Myself First

(The government had announced that churches would be permitted to reopen for public worship from July 4th 2020 but it took time for parishes to make the necessary adjustments)

I wonder would it seem strange after all our time of isolation if I tried to convince you of the importance of silence. Silence is as vital as oxygen in our lives. It is the wind beneath our wings when we are rising and doing well; it is the safety net beneath the tightrope we are walking when we fall. And still it will be new to many of us because our lives are lived 'on the outside' for the most part. Yet in reality, ninety-nine per cent of our living goes on 'on the inside'. That is where we are and where we live. Everything that goes on outside has to be dealt with by us on the inside. It is where the pressure builds and so it requires our daily attention.

We are trying to keep ourselves balanced on the tightrope of daily demands such as home schooling, working from home, caring for elderly parents—not to mention the deadly isolation that is common to all of us. Ironically, the age of Zoom and social media is not always a great help because everything is reduced to slogans and headlines. A conversation in real time and space is what we are all missing.

We could go through life and never really meet ourselves. So could I invite you to come home to yourself? At first, it will feel like a waste of time. You could be doing so many useful things that need to be done. The desire to switch on the TV or radio, to listen to music or a sound of some kind will distract you. You will feel like the fellow trying to give up the fags, the alcoholic giving up the booze or the addict coming off the drugs. This is because we have been drugged on noise and activity all our lives and silence will give us real withdrawal symptoms. Do not be surprised. It is normal for us to feel this way at the beginning. Persevere and you will find *'a peace the world cannot give' (John 14:27).*

This time of crisis is an opportunity, as we talk of 'return', to let each one of us come back to ourselves. It will be the best thing we can do to enrich our parish community. But it must be a daily commitment. There is no quick fix. You are a wonderful person, well worth meeting and spending a little time with for a daily visit. And your heart and soul need that daily visit from you more than from anybody else!

So sit comfortably. Be aware of your posture and what you are thinking and feeling. Be aware of your breathing, hearing and sensing. Try it for ten minutes to begin with. You will slowly come home to yourself and God will be very near. You have to come to meet yourself and God is there, too!

We are going back to church
but it will not be the same
as the one we left
four months ago

Going Back to Church

(Two weeks after the announcement that churches could open for public worship, all the requirements were in place and although social distancing restrictions would limit numbers, the parish was about to come together for Mass for the first time since March)

We are going back to church, but it will not be the same as the one we left four months ago. That church and that world are gone and we are now in a very different Church and a different world. So we must be people of faith and resist the natural temptation to hanker after the past and the familiar. A lot has happened since March. Christ has risen and gone ahead of us into Galilee.

We must move on together. At the outset, we thought it would be a short-term situation and things would soon return to the way they were. Now we know it won't be, and it probably shouldn't be. So what challenge does this situation present to Christianity, to the Church, to you and to me? When Pope Francis says that the Church should be a 'field hospital', he means not in isolation from the world but being with the people where they are physically and mentally, socially and spiritually, in their affliction. This is the Galilee Jesus told us he has gone to and we will find him there and recognise him by his wounds.

Like any good hospital, the Church also has a preventive role and it is here we all have an urgent part to play. The Church must diagnose the malignant viruses spreading all over the Body of Christ in our society today, where fear, hatred, populism and nationalism are rife. We must recognise this and replace it with a healing acceptance of each person as being one of God's family and so one of our own. It is a beautiful thing to see the many signs of this all around us since lockdown.

Where do we go from here and how do we begin? Let us start at home in our own hearts. I am writing this reflection on Wednesday and this morning's Prayer of the Church has the following prayers:

1. We give thanks to Christ and we praise him because he calls us his brothers and sisters.
2. Help us to live the new life of Easter so that people may know through us the power of your love.
3. Every day is proof of your love. As you bring us to this new day, make us new in mind and heart.
4. Teach us to see you present in all people. Help us to recognise you most of all in those who suffer.
5. May our lives today be filled with your compassion. Give us a spirit of forgiveness and a generous heart.[1]

How lovely it would be if each one of us could make these prayers our own, praying them every morning with a genuine desire for them to be answered through us as we go about our daily lives. It is practical and something we can all do—and it is a place to begin.

---

1. *The Divine Office Psalter,* Week 1, Wednesday morning intercessions

The Avenue of Trees

We returned to church last Sunday and I found it a moving experience in many ways. Some changes felt very strange and will take time, such as keeping our social distance and having to wear facemasks. You will be looking at your friend and not recognising them until they speak. I know this will work itself out as we find ways to improve each week. These are the things I think about as I take my daily exercise.

Walking up the towering, majestic Avenue of Trees near Acklam Hall and passing under their protective shelter is a beautiful experience for me. I can hear the trees discussing among themselves this recent arrival on the planet—a tiny creature, not even a hundred years old, who doesn't usually even live that long. They point to the sky and seem to say to me, *'Look up at the scorching sun and get your life into some perspective.'*

I look up at the sky and see this big burning morning sun and wonder what it sees when it looks down on me and my surroundings. I visualise what it must have seen a thousand years ago on this day, or five thousand or a hundred thousand or even five million years ago!

Then I wonder what it will see down here in another thousand years, or five thousand or a hundred thousand or even five million years from now on the anniversary of this day. Now I review the various stages of my life: infancy, childhood, adolescence, adulthood, middle age, reflecting on the things that once seemed so important, that caused me worry and anxiety, things I clung stubbornly to, things I thought I could never live with—or live without. Looking back from the distance of today, I ask myself, *'How many of those dreams and fears are in me now?'*

Then I review some of the problems I have today: my present worries, sufferings, fears and anxieties, and of each of them I say, *'These, too, will pass away.'* I think of things I cling to or that I am possessive of now and I realise a day will come when I shall see them differently, when of each of these attachments I will surely say, *'These, too, will pass away.'*

And so I continue on my way to the end of these beautiful, wise trees, thanking them for drawing me out of myself and plunging me deeper into myself at the same time. They have helped me once again, like so many times in the past, to see myself in context and to see the bigger picture.

Peter Goes for a Walk on the Water

St Peter is walking on the water this Sunday. Have you ever tried it? It's a tricky business, although there may have been moments in our lives when we have felt like we could. Maybe some of us might even recall a time when we felt like we had actually achieved it—metaphorically speaking, that is!

The reality is we are all walking on water with every step we take and there is a loving Father providing us with life and breath for every moment. Not only that, but each of us also has a protector and guide watching over us, whom we call our guardian angel. This is a divine presence to accompany us as we journey through our every day. How special we must be in the sight of our Heavenly Father! Of course, we don't ever think of ourselves in this way, nor should we (not for too long, anyway), but it does us no harm to reflect on this reality every now and again.

But what about when we are sinking? We all know those moments, too. The worries and cares, the knocks and disappointments, the frustrations and annoyances, the bereavements and health scares, the breakdowns and break-ups in all their different varieties. The list goes on and on. Someone must have reached out in some way to lend a helping hand because we have survived and we are still here. Not only that, but when we look back, we know we have grown and become better versions of ourselves. We are more aware of others and their concerns. We are more compassionate and dare I say we might even have a little more wisdom. All of this comes at a price of course, and we have the scars and wounds to show for it—just as Our Lord and Saviour had before us.

Yes indeed, we are all walking on the water with you, Peter! So can we ask you to be our support in the storms of life and bring us all safely to the shore?

The Assumption of Our Lady

Mary is the woman for our time and the woman for all seasons. She was homeless for the birth of her first born and had to flee to a foreign country as an asylum seeker, for the protection of his life. She was a hurt and confused young mother when he was only twelve years old and got lost in the temple. She was the caring, discreet one at the wedding who noticed the embarrassment of a family who had run out of wine and quietly reported it to Jesus, knowing he could help. She stood at the foot of the cross, helpless to do anything, yet giving him strength just by her presence. And as for her faith, she believed through all of this and everything in between that God was working out his plan. She had said her 'Yes' and lived it out.

We all know what a beautiful thing it is to see the personal traits and qualities of parents living in their children. What better form of devotion to Our Lady could we give her than to allow some of her personal qualities to take root and grow in each one of us? We all have it in us to put a smile of pride on the face of our Heavenly Mother as she delights in her children on earth every day.

Happy Assumption Day!

It is a good time to reflect
on where we have come from
and what we have learned
and discovered about ourselves
over these past months

Wisdom Stories

(Rising infection rates had prompted the government to remove the 'travel corridor' for several countries and re-impose a fourteen-day self-isolation requirement for people returning to the UK)

Simple little stories this week, yet full of wisdom. You may find food and nourishment, depending on how much you wish to look back over your own personal experience. Apart from entertainment value, there is a deeper meaning when we reflect on them. In the words of Jesus, the stories are the wineskins containing the good wine. They are about what is going on in our own lives.

The first story is of a monk living out in the desert. He was tormented by the fact he could no longer reflect and meditate as he once had and when he could bear it no longer, he decided to abandon his cell and go somewhere else. As he was putting on his sandals to carry out his resolve, he saw another monk not far from where he stood, who was also putting his sandals on.

'Who are you?' he asked the stranger.

'I am your self,' was the reply. 'If it is on my account you are leaving this place, I would have you know that no matter where you go I shall go with you.'

What you are running away from and what you yearn for are all within you!

And here's another little one...

Said the despairing client to the psychiatrist: *'No matter where I go, I have to take myself along—and it spoils everything.'*

What you are running from is always within you!

These little stories in my own experience carry such a truth. I have lost count of the number of times I have tried to get away from it all, only to find that my problems come with me. I go on holiday only to find that as I get off the plane I am there to meet myself at the airport with all my same problems. And don't you feel for all those thousands of our brothers and sisters who have set out on their holidays to France or Spain and now Croatia, only for Boris and EasyJet to suddenly pull the plug? Now they have to rush back home and join the queue at the airports. Not much of a holiday!

The lesson for us all—happiness is an inside job.

A Word with the Housebound, Elderly and Grandparents

(Although shops, cafes, churches and other venues had been open for some time, Covid continued to claim lives and many elderly and vulnerable people were continuing to stay at home)

I know many of you may feel the world is too fast, too changed, for you to have an active part in your family life or the parish community. You may worry there is nothing you can do to support your children and grandchildren. I want to tell you that nothing could be further from the truth. In fact now is your time and this is your season because what you have to offer is exactly what every family and every community needs right now. You have faith in abundance and a vast store of wisdom. Some of this will have been passed on to you from your good parents and grandparents, freely and without charge, while more will have been acquired through the painful cost of your own lived experience. For the younger generation, finding their way through life in these confusing times can be frightening and you are a real shining light for them, showing the way, more than you will ever realise.

I can speak from personal experience over the past few months about the power of your prayer. It was your prayers through the grace of God that brought me through this difficult time. For this reason I can speak with authority in telling you what a powerful role you play in our families and parish. Be you grandparents, elderly or housebound, you are the engines supplying wisdom and the transmitters supplying faith to the generations following you. This is your great gift to the community. You are needed now more than ever and don't ever forget that.

You are the very people who can change the world. Through your love and faithful intercession you are investing into a 'piggy bank' of prayer, which your children and grandchildren's guardian angels will call upon in times of need. You are saving away—not a penny a day or a pound a day, but a prayer a day. That is the gift that cannot be bought and it is priceless. I will leave the last word to Pope Francis:

'In a special way, old age is a time of grace, in which the Lord renews his call to us: he calls us to safeguard and transmit the faith: he calls us to pray, especially to intercede... Grandparents, who have received the blessing of seeing their children's children (cf Psalm 128:6), *are entrusted with a great responsibility: to convey their life experience, their family history, the history of a community, of a people and to share with simplicity their wisdom and faith which is the most precious legacy! Blessed are those families who have grandparents close by!'*[1]

---

1. Address of Pope Francis at his meeting with the elderly in St Peter's Square on Sunday September 28th 2014

Switching on My Radio

When I switch on my radio or TV these days, the topic of conversation very often seems to be about depression or mental health. I find it particularly disturbing that the discussion has now turned to the mental health of our children.

Of course, we are all well aware of the pressures on ourselves and our families at this time. None of us are without problems and anxieties of some kind, but I wonder if there could be something more to this. Is it because too few of us have been sufficiently affirmed that we are seeing these problems now? I often wonder whether we could have been more generous in our praise of one another. I am asking myself and you the same question: can you remember a time in your life when a significant elder, such as your father, your mother, a teacher, a priest, your boss, an aunt or an uncle took a true delight in you—your energies, your talents, your ideas, or just you as a person? Can you remember a time when you heard a significant person in your life tell you that you delighted them? For many people this may never have happened, or if it did, only in a few fleeting moments. And if this is the case, is it any wonder so many of us are depressed? If no one is regularly lifting the constricting cloud from our hearts and souls, they can never swell with joy and gratitude. Of course, many of us have been blessed with wonderful people who have praised us and built us up and perhaps even continue to do so. Those we remember and give thanks for! Reflecting on our own experience might lead us to ask a further question of ourselves: when was the last time I walked across a room to praise another person, young or old? This may be as big a revelation as the first question. But this is one we can now do something about. For when we praise another person then our own hearts will fill with exuberance and God will not be far away.

So many times at Mass, we recite the Response to the Psalm, *'The Lord takes delight in his people' (Psalm 149).* If it is true that the Lord takes delight in us, calls us friends *(John 15:15)*, tells us we are the salt of the earth *(Matthew 5:13)* and the light of the world *(Matthew 5:14)*, then it would seem only natural that he would want us to do the same with those around us—and tell them so.

Entering the Next Stage of the Pandemic

(Social gatherings of more than six people were now illegal)

As we are entering the next stage of the pandemic, this might be a good time to reflect on where we have come from and what we have learned about ourselves over these past months. There were all those things we took for granted and now we see as luxuries. The loveliness of each person and the beauty of family life are the grace of God among us. We are catching a glimpse of that now while we have the time to reflect on what we once had and for the moment, is being taken from us. This, along with all the other things we miss, will be given back to us again and received with new appreciation and gratitude in our hearts. Hopefully, we will all end up much better people for this experience. In the meantime we can take the opportunity for a serious reflection.

On 27th March, in an empty St Peter's Square, Pope Francis, addressing the Lord in prayer, said:

'The coronavirus is not a time of your judgement, but of our judgement, a time to separate what matters and what passes away, a time to choose what is necessary from what is not. It is a time to put our lives back on track with regard to you, Lord, and to others.'

These words call us all to reflect on our situation before the pandemic—where we were, what values we upheld and our way of life. You could say we lived in a bubble, cocooned in our consumerist culture. Our artificially created needs gave us an overproduction of goods. These were aggressively advertised to convey the illusion of fulfilment, happiness, success. If we stand together with the Lord and look back at where we were and how we were living, we can see it more clearly now. Our world was predictable. We felt undisturbed, tranquil and in control. There was a world out there where terrible wars were taking place and people were fleeing their countries and homes, but that was all far away in other lands—although some asylum seekers were coming among us. We were being asked to look beyond ourselves to other parts of the world, and to the planet itself. A change was slowly taking place but the sudden, sharp experience of the Covid-19 virus left us in turmoil.

Sadly, our religious knowledge had not always grown in line with our lived experience, so religion became marginalised. What could have been our guide to direct us in these troubled times had been abandoned and discarded as irrelevant in our culture and time. We could no longer see where our society was heading and how fast. Our new identity was defined by possessions, prestige and performance, and the redemption they promised was taking the place of our churches, which were already emptying long before this crisis.

Because our lives were so fast and so busy, we had been pushed into the fast lane against our will and had to try to survive there. This meant our lives had to be lived on the surface, with little or no time or space for ourselves. The occasional personal or family crisis would take us a little deeper into ourselves and we drew strength from a place we had not known to be in there—a strength we didn't know we had. This turmoil may well turn out to be a blessing and do us a great favour. Let us seize this opportunity and reflect on what we can leave behind and what we can bring with us on our journey. Some of the baggage society tells us we must carry may not be necessary at all and it's high time we dropped it. On the other hand, there is so much that is rich and nourishing for our lives—family, community and the world around us—that we may have been losing our grip on. Now is the time for us to judge what is necessary and what is not.

My Desire for Our Whole Parish

Now that we are into autumn, I have decided to write a reflection this week on the colder days and longer nights that lie ahead. Listening to the news these days is making us realise we are all in this pandemic for the long haul and that means we are to be cocooned for much longer than we had been hoping. It seems we may even have to go through the whole of the winter in this way and that has made me think about how we are to make sure we look after all those people in our community who live alone and are housebound, many of whom will be feeling isolated and vulnerable.

Our community is blessed with wonderful folk who are reaching out to people in so many ways: updating the census, acting as stewards for those coming to Mass, putting the newsletter together, knocking on doors just to say hello, doing shopping and taking the newspaper to folk, phoning for a chat or supporting the food bank. And I'm writing my little reflections while many of you are taking them to people who cannot access email or Facebook. These are all signs of God working in and through us—the leaven in the dough—and I know that much more is going on behind the scenes.

But now I am asking myself if there is something more we could be doing together and whether we might be able to share these things out between us. I am sure we are still not connecting with many of our vulnerable friends and also families who may well be struggling and might appreciate a link up. Wouldn't it be great if we could mobilise the whole parish so that everybody feels responsible and we all play our part to ensure nobody is forgotten or isolated?

How lovely it would be if every one of us could seek out even one of those people living close by who might appreciate a knock on the door and seeing a friendly face. You could drop off a newspaper or tell them about Mass in our church or on YouTube. Anything that connects us during this period of isolation is vital because we all need to feel that we belong. To begin with I would like to see our parish newsletter and weekly reflection going out to as many people as possible and I can only do that with your help.

If we can do this we can change the face of the earth in our area. Then the good Lord will have done his usual work again and will turn this terrible virus into a huge success story in our street and our area but as always, he needs our hands and feet and voices. I have no doubt he can trust each one of our community to play their part. With the Lord on our side and being together, far from fearing the days ahead, we can all look forward to them with joy and confidence.

They took centuries to write
so the words in the psalms
carry the faith and despair
of generations.
These are prayers
from the heart.

Reflecting on Psalm 79(80)

The Vineyard of the Lord is the House of Israel

By equipping ourselves with a little more knowledge about the psalms, we can find rich nourishment for our own souls. So I thought we might reflect on the psalms. They took centuries to write, so the words in them carry the faith and despair of generations. They are prayers from the heart—in fact, they are very gutsy at times. I have included questions along the way because it is only by putting our own lived experience into the psalm that we understand it, when it fits us like our own clothes. Put yourself beside the author and feel his heartbeat, watch his tears, enjoy his laughter and join in his praise. It is when you can say, 'I feel like that sometimes too', that you are praying the psalm.

You brought a vine out of Egypt; *[Who brought you along your journey of life?]*

To plant it you drove out the nations. It stretched out its branches to the sea, *[Who can you be yourself with?]*

to the Great River it stretched out its shoots. Then why have you broken down its walls? *[Then why do we have this Covid-19?]*

It is plucked by all who pass by. It is ravaged by the boar of the forest, *[What is draining you at the present time?]*

devoured by the beasts of the field. *[Do you ever feel overcome and spent?]*

God of hosts, turn again, we implore, look down from heaven and see. Visit this vine and protect it, *[Lord, we need you now. Have you ever said this?]*

the vine your right hand has planted. And we shall never forsake you again; *[Have you ever said, 'I'll never do that again?']*

give us life that we may call upon your name. God of hosts, bring us back; let your face shine on us and we shall be saved.

Reflecting on Psalm 22(23)

We believe in the Incarnation—God the Son has come down from heaven and taken on our flesh so he can be with us in this way. This is the very heart of our faith. It can be uncomfortable that he is this close and so it is not surprising that the great temptation is to dis-incarnate Jesus again and return him to heaven. We all do this in our imaginations, probably because it makes life more comfortable and we won't be on trial every day with our words and movements. But the fact is that Jesus is living his life again now in you and in me, and in every person on this planet. '*Whatever you did to the least of these of these... you did to me' (Matthew 25:40).* All is very clear and challenging.

The Good News is today's Responsorial Psalm, The Lord is my Shepherd. He is shepherding you and me now in all those lovely people in our lives—and strangers, too. In order to locate the Good Shepherd in my own life I have included some questions for myself and I share them with you. Answering these, or any other questions that may arise in you, will make the psalm as personal for you as it is for the author and you will uncover the Good Shepherd in your own life.

The Lord is my shepherd; there is nothing I shall want. *[Who makes you feel secure?]*

Fresh and green are the pastures where he gives me repose. *[In what way do they do this?]*

Near restful waters he leads me, *[How do you find their company restful and life-giving?]*

to revive my drooping spirit *[Have they picked you up when you were low?]*

He guides me along the right path; he is true to his name. *[Do you confide in them at times of need?]*

If I should walk in the valley of darkness, no evil would I fear. *[How do they give you courage when you are anxious or frightened?]*

You are there with your crook and your staff; *[Is it with their words or simply being in their company?]*

with these you give me comfort. *[In what other ways do they comfort you?]*

You have prepared a banquet for me *[How is life a celebration because of these lovely people?]*

In the sight of my foes. *[In spite of all the difficulties?]*

My head you have anointed with oil; *[How do you know they love you?]*

my cup is overflowing. *[What makes your heart fill with gratitude?]*

Surely goodness and kindness shall follow me *[I am surrounded with goodness]*

all the days of my life. *[Always and everywhere I go]*

In the Lord's own house shall I dwell *[Because God's house is the whole of creation!]*

for ever and ever. *[And I am there now, in this life and in the next]*

Reflecting on Psalm 17 (18)

Psalm 17(18) is a long one but we only have the first and last verse at Mass this Sunday. It is a psalm of praise sung by King David as he looks back on his life and recognises that God has been his constant protector and guide.

Sit yourself down beside King David and listen to him singing this psalm. He sings every line with feeling because they are the events of the ups and downs in his life. God has carried David through them all and he is so aware of this that all he wants to do is sing praise and thanks to his God. Since David's time, God has come to us in the flesh. So now he is coming to you in mysterious ways as he did for David, but he also comes in the flesh of those around you. Go through each line with David and fill it in with the mystery of events in your life and see how God is touching you through the people who surround you every day.

Hitchhiking on King David's Shoulders

I love you, Lord, my strength, *[How is the Lord your strength?]* my rock, my fortress, my saviour. *[Who is the rock solid one for you in your life?]*

My God is the rock where I take refuge; *[Any incidents when you took refuge in God or a trusted friend?]*

my shield, my mighty help, my stronghold. *[Who are any of these for you?]*

The Lord is worthy of all praise. *[What would you want to praise God for?]*

when I call I am saved from my foes. *[Who can and do you call on for help?]*

Long life to the Lord, my rock! *[With whom do you raise a glass and say, 'Good health'?]*

Praised be the God who saves me. *[Have there been times you were afraid?]*

He has given great victories to his king *[What are your moments of relief or achievement?]*

and shown his love for his anointed. *[When are the times you have felt love from God or another person?]*

How lovely it is to know
we are still linked
with our loved ones
who have died,
that we can still connect
and go on living with them

Why All Saints Day?

There are many reasons for All Saints Day. We can reflect on a few, and how they touch us in our lives. There are so many lovely people who have influenced us from as far back as we can remember and indeed continue to do so. When they died, they did not go away, they only went to God and he is always with us. Their dying was like Christ's dying and rising, which means they are alive now with God. They are forever with us (as God is). We all have moments when we experience something of this but cannot find words to express it. Yet we know nothing is more real because we can feel that connection and their presence.

The Church is so much more than just those of us here on earth. We are but a tiny portion. The Church is also composed of the whole company of heaven—all those who have ever lived since the very beginning of life on earth. This is where we are anchored. These are our real strength and our security, with the apostles and prophets as our foundation stone. They are all very much with us and from their place in heaven they are constantly interceding for us. Each of us will be mentioned frequently by name to our Heavenly Father by our loved ones, just as they did when they were here with us. They continue to carry and support us as they always have done.

Another good reason for this day is to take the opportunity to reflect on our parish and indeed every parish. The first thing we will notice is that every parish is different; each has its own 'personality'. This is the legacy of those who were in this place before us. They lived, loved, laughed and cried; they tried their best. They would fall, get up and try again. They all worshipped together in this place and they still do today. That is why we say at Mass: '...so now we join with all the company of heaven as we say...' It is for real. They are all here with us at Mass. This is too much to understand, yet not too much for our awareness.

Yes, there is so much more to the Church than the visible, just as there is so much more to you and me than the visible. Our loved ones have not gone anywhere but to God, and God is very near. The feast of All Saints is here to give us the opportunity to brush up our *awareness* of this wonderful company that surrounds us every day.

Praying for the Dead

November is the month of the Holy Souls and a good time to think about what we mean by praying for our loved ones who have died. This reflection is meant as an aid to help us to be with our own loved ones who have gone ahead of us—nothing more. The time we spend with these this month is personal and sacred. And because of Christ's dying and rising, our faith is that they all share, in Christ, that same dying and rising. Although we cannot fully understand it all, we can catch glimpses by being able to contact them with Christ in prayer and being aware of their presence with us. All of this is a cause of great consolation to us and a huge boost to our faith. We are with them together and forever.

But why do we pray for those who have died? What good does it do? Is it to remind God to be merciful? No. God needs no reminders. Is it to ask God to see a heart of gold beneath the failings and shortcomings? God doesn't need a lesson from us on understanding. A cynic might ask, 'Why pray for the dead because if they are in heaven they don't need our prayers and if they are in hell, our prayers won't be of any help?' These are valid questions that rise up inside of us. And strangely enough, when we reflect on our own experience, it is inside ourselves, too, that we will find many answers. Only in this way can we make some sense of this tradition we have of praying for the dead.

So what is our experience? We pray for the dead because we want to. It does us good; we feel the need, and that is reason enough. Prayer changes us, not God. Prayer is meant to console us. We pray for the dead to comfort ourselves, to stir our own faith and at times to ease our own guilt about our less-than-perfect relationship with the one who has died, although in most cases we have no need to feel guilty at all. We have been heroic and generous and the one who has died is truly grateful for the support we gave.

We pray for the dead because we are still in vital communion with them. We can still feel that flow of life between them and us. *'The ties of love and affection do not unravel at death' (Catholic funeral liturgy).* We can feel this. We love and console each other. Not only that, but our relationship continues to deepen, change and develop with time just as it did when they were alive. Although we cannot explain this, it is something that is going on inside us.

So we pray for the dead in order to keep in contact with them. Just as we hold someone's hand when they are dying, which can be an immense consolation to them and to us, we can figuratively (but it is just as real), hold that person's hand through and beyond death. All of this is what we feel in our gut and in our heart and this is what is meant by the doctrine of the Communion of Saints. It is actually what is going on in us when we lose a loved one.

So when we look for answers to our religious questions, we do well not to go to the 'expert'. The answers are to be found in ourselves. Praying for our dead is a case in point, where reflecting on our experience and what we find ourselves thinking, feeling and doing is the best teacher and we know it is true.

How Are We to Understand Purgatory?

I must say at the start, when we speak of purgatory, we are all speaking like blind folk trying to imagine the scenery. All we have to rely on is our limited experience without sight and the words of our guide. For any understanding of a purgatory that speaks to us, then, we need firstly to have some experience of it in our own lives, and secondly to keep in step with the Scriptures, especially Jesus and the New Testament.

Let me introduce you to little Ted. He is not yet two years old and not only is he walking, but he has discovered where the biscuits are kept. Though his mammy tells him not to take any, he can't resist. His mammy catches him in the act and hugs him with delight and pride. Yet little Ted cries. In the embrace of love he knows and feels he should have been better—a purgatory moment? And he will have many more before he is two unless the biscuits are put out of reach!

Which one of us hasn't had moments in our lives when we have felt dissatisfied with the way we have behaved? We knew we could have been better. We have been mean, petty and small, all the while knowing we are much better than our behaviour has been. But there have been other times when we have spent the evening with delightful company, beautiful people, and we were at our very best. We came away so energised, filled with life and wanting to be a better person. Could these be purgatory moments?

The scriptures are peppered with pictures that open up the purgatory experience to us. The Prodigal Son in the embrace of his father: *'We are going to have a feast, a celebration' (Luke 15:23).* The woman brought before Jesus is to be stoned to death: *'Neither do I condemn you, go and sin no more' (John 8:11).* St Peter at the great catch of fish: *'Leave me Lord, I am a sinful man' (Luke 5:8).* After his denial, Jesus looks at him with forgiveness: *'He went outside and wept bitterly' (Luke 22:62).* Zacchaeus: *'If I have cheated anyone, I will pay back four times the amount' (Luke 19:8).* These are all purgatory moments, when we are aware of our sin yet loved unconditionally and it makes us want to be a better version of ourselves.

Our funeral Mass tells us, *'When our bodies lie in death, we gain an everlasting place in heaven.'* That would indicate we go straight to heaven and so the pain of purgatory will be something to do with joining a loving God and the company of heaven in our imperfect state. Being in this company will make us want to change more, as we have done so many times in our lives already and become the best version of ourselves. Put simply, this is what God made you and me for—to be our *true selves* and to be together with him forever. Like little Ted, his mother's pride and joy, we know this is only a dim reflection of our Heavenly Father's delight in all of us.

Communion of Saints

Our Great Comfort and Consolation

This is one of the most consoling doctrines of our faith. It is no wonder the Church gives us November to enjoy our privileged position in their company. How lovely it is to know we are still linked with our loved ones who have died, that we can still connect and go on living with them. Even if it is in a different state, our relationship with them is ongoing, as we are all imperfect. This is important for all of us to know. And because we are imperfect, so are our relationships.

Often when people die, they have family and loved ones around them. That is the ideal. But not everyone gets to die that way. People die through war, accidents, suicide, heart attack, drug overdose, stroke, violence, hunger and poverty. People die unforgiven and unforgiving—not fully reconciled. It is not unusual for death to catch us before we have had time to say the things we should have said and done the things we should have done. Too often, we die with unfinished business. We need forgiveness for what we have done and failed to do.

Who among us doesn't have unfinished business with someone whom death has taken away? Maybe a hurt inflicted or received? Or we feel guilt, because while that person was alive, we should have given more of ourselves but we were too busy with our own lives at the time. Worse still, it may have been someone with whom we'd had a disagreement. We should have made some gesture of reconciliation but never did. Death has separated us and now we have to live with the guilt, wishing we had done something before it was too late.

But it's not too late! Not if we take seriously the Christian doctrine of the Communion of Saints. We stand and profess it every Sunday at Mass, but do we believe and feel it in our guts and our heart? This is really important because we continue to be in the one community of life with those who have died. They walk with us, as Jesus walked with the two disciples on the road to Emmaus and they sit at table with us, as Jesus did with those disciples. And all this is because their dying is just like Jesus' dying—it was a dying and rising to a new way of living.

Here lies the Good News for us all. There is still time *after* death for reconciliation and healing—on both sides—because inside the Communion of Saints we have privileged access to each other. We know this is true because we experience it. And here we can speak all those words we couldn't speak before; we can reach across death's divide.

It can be a great consolation to die a happy death in the arms of love with no unfinished business. But happily, there's time still after death for this to happen for those of us who are not so lucky. The bond between us continues, grows and develops. We know this, we feel and experience it in our hearts and souls. The doctrine of the Communion of Saints reassures us that what is going on in us is true.

Our Support Team Through Lockdown

The pandemic has been a difficult time for so many and yet as the days have gone by, I discovered it has had one redeeming quality. It forced us into 'lockdown' and 'social distancing' and as a result, there has been space around us for others to come in and fill. To my surprise, I found myself immediately invaded by a most delightful gathering. They were coming with stories, songs, laughter and entertainment. They knew nothing about lockdown or social distancing, but made sure I would not feel alone, lonely and isolated.

These were the ones we call the Communion of Saints, although I wouldn't put them all into that tidy category myself. Some were, no doubt, but others were lovely rogues and mischief makers, up to every joke and trick they could find and that's why I always enjoyed their company so much; they were life-givers. We refer to them often as the Faithful

Departed, but I knew this month they have not departed at all. A lot may have changed from the way we used to touch and communicate with them, of course it has. But they are still very much alive and in our company all the time.

Along with the obvious ones—family, friends and neighbours—there were so many others as well. They didn't so much come to me as they were with me *all* the time, wherever I went—outside, inside, in bed, in the kitchen, in the living room—and like all my best friends, I couldn't shake them off! I could hear their usual conversations as they repeated the same stories and we laughed heartily as though hearing them for the first time. Of course we sang so many of our familiar songs together with gusto. They joined me on every walk and here we had quieter conversations about the deeper things going on in us. I found this so comforting that I often continued walking for longer, as I didn't want to leave their company.

The dreams were the best, as they obey no logic. Time and space means nothing and so there are no limitations. Here again, as well as family and neighbours, I was joined by friends I had never even met in my life yet I knew them well, as they had given me such great pleasure in their lives. Dreams are good for name dropping! Terry Wogan joined me one night and Muhammad Ali entertained me on another occasion. I was having a very interesting conversation with Big Jack Charlton about his glory days with the Irish soccer team and I asked how he felt being adored as the King of Hearts and High King of Ireland. Alex Ferguson then walked in on the conversation and I woke up. He had destroyed my lovely dream—as he has done for so many of my dreams!

This God,
creator and centre of everything,
was carried for nine months
by a peasant woman
in Palestine - and he continues
to come into our world
in every new baby who is born

What is the Point of Advent?

This is intended as a simple aid to help us distinguish the promptings of the Spirit from the other wonderful ones that are all around us as we head up to Christmas. I hope you survive the rush and continue to have a wonderful Advent.

Five-year-old Andrew tells me that Advent means lots of more sleeps to Christmas—a very long time! But what is Advent for the adult? For some, it will be exciting and full of anticipation. For others, it will be an anxious and stressful time with financial worries as they prepare for Christmas. Yet deep in every heart there is something else going on. This is because our Creator has put an ache in us that occasionally comes to the surface. We can confuse this ache with loneliness because on the surface it feels that way, but in reality it is completely different.

Advent is a time for us to focus on this aspect of ourselves and to distinguish what is surface aching which, though very real, can be dealt with in various ways—a little retail therapy, a trip to the pub or the cinema, a chat with a friend and so on. But where there is a deeper ache, God is calling for our attention. It is important that we recognise this and get some time and space to be alone with him—not always easy with the demands of a family. Yet here we can learn from Jesus. The busier he was, the more he needed to find a lonely place where he could be alone with his Father.

Although happy with our lives, we are always longing for something more. We are made like this by our God, for him and his kingdom. We are all citizens of eternity, yet living and confined by this small human condition. We don't fit comfortably here and deep down we know there is so much more to us.

Advent is here to point out our condition and help us to see it for ourselves. Then we can find a way forward by dealing with surface longings and those deeper longings in the appropriate ways, leading to a much fuller and more rewarding life.

Returning to little Andrew, he is already experiencing these longings, waiting for something big to come. He will have hair on his chest before he understands what is going on in him and what it is all about. That's why we have the season of Advent.

Christmas Symbols

Christmas symbols are over-commercialised, it is true. But why complain if shops put up colourful lights to celebrate the birth of Christ and God's presence in the world? Rejoice and sing with the angels! Raise a glass too, as the baby liked to do when he grew up.

The Crèche is an image of heaven. Everything about it radiates peace, love, fulfilment, the end of all longing. The baby is usually asleep and as we hear the words of the beautiful carol Silent Night, '*Sleep in heavenly peace*', the song and the picture combined are as good a picture of heaven as you can get on this side of eternity.

The Crib is a trough, a place where cows and sheep come to eat. It is appropriate that Jesus—the food of life for the world—should be lying on a trough, and a wooden one too. The wood of the crib will later become the wood of the cross.

The Christmas Tree's job is to join heaven and earth. God is with us, not above us, but with a larger quality of life. We enjoy a portion of it now and we are on the way to the fullness of that life.

The Christmas Lights originated in the northern hemisphere where it is dark and cold at this time of year. The idea then is that when it is darkest and coldest in our own lives and in our world, God's light and warmth breaks through.

The Christmas Carols—what are they doing and saying? They celebrate our joy at Jesus' birth and we also join with the song of the angels at the first and at every Christmas.

Wonder—Ponder—Be Amazed!

(The government had initially planned to allow up to three households to meet together over the Christmas period, but after the emergence of a new strain of the Covid virus, a 'Christmas bubble' would be permitted to meet for Christmas Day only. Parts of Britain in 'Tier 4' could not meet with anyone outside of their household)

I often wonder if we have domesticated God in our Christmas celebrations and liturgies. The baby in the manger is the starting place and that is enough for the children to focus on. However, adults will be expected to move beyond that. This is God who holds the whole universe in the palm of his hand. Yet he has become a weak and vulnerable newborn baby in order to get close to us. If we struggle to take in his Creation, which we all do, how can we take in the mystery of the Creator as a newborn baby lying on a bed of straw? Nevertheless, as much as that should lead us to wonder, ponder and be amazed, we must not stay at the Crib!

Five-year-old Rosie tells the Christmas story like this: *'They were so poor they only had butter for their sandwiches and they went a long way from home without getting lost. The lady rode a donkey, the man walked and the baby was inside the lady. They had to stay in a stable with an ox and an ass. But the three rich men found them because a star lit the roof. Shepherds came and you could pet the sheep but not feed them. Then the baby was born. And do you know who he was? The baby was God.'*

What a wild and unbelievable statement! The Creator of the universe is born as a baby into our world. This is *'Christmas for adults'* from now on, so stay with me and let us imagine the universe. Light travels at 186,000 miles per second. It takes little more than a second to get from the moon to the earth, and from the sun to earth it takes about eight minutes. These are among our close neighbours and yet the distance is immense. But in terms of the universe it is tiny.

Now take the stars in the sky. The closest ones to us take over four years for their light to reach us and 800,000 years for the furthest away (and remember the speed of light). And there are billions and trillions of them. Is it all too much for our minds? Yes, of course, it is! But now try to imagine at the centre of all this is our Creator who made it all and who guides each of these stars and planets daily. Not only that, but right now he is watching over us so that not a hair falls from your head or mine without him knowing and caring.

Yet this God, creator and centre of everything, was actually carried for nine months by a peasant woman in Palestine. He was born into our world as a baby and then lived here, taught us and gave us all the powers he himself had as God. He has spilled the fullness of his life into each one of us. And he continues to come into our world in every new baby who is born. It all seems too good to be true. Sure, it's no wonder we will be singing songs, sharing presents and passing drinks around our 'Christmas bubbles.'

Nothing Has Changed

I recently read an article by Father Bryan Massingale of the Archdiocese of Milwaukee, in which he described the Christmas story as being *'hauntingly relevant'* to the current situation regarding asylum seekers. He was aware that some might object to this *'politicising of the gospel'*, but pointed out that Mary, Joseph and their baby would not have been among the kind of immigrants a nation would consider desirable. On the contrary, the infant Jesus was regarded as *'a threat to national security'*.

The Christmas story is that nothing has changed. When we consider the gospel accounts of Christ's birth in Bethlehem and his family's struggle for survival, only then will we be able to see him in that struggle now. Every time we look at our newspapers or turn on the news, the Bethlehem Story is unfolding before our eyes. God is coming into the world in every child that is born. That is the dignity of every person. And it is our identity as human beings. Each one of us now is God made flesh. That is what we celebrate. Christmas is for adults. The crib and the baby are for children, until they grow up and become adult Christians.

Father Massingale suggests that as we put up our cribs this Christmas, we should of course reflect on the events of long ago, but perhaps we might also place around the crib images of those who are being persecuted throughout the world, and those who have to be separated from their loved ones and their homeland: children, parents, grandparents and relatives. And perhaps we might pray for wealthy nations whose policies, he suggests, '*are crueller than those of biblical Egypt*'.[1]

---

1. *US Catholic* magazine, December 5th 2019

We pray for a new year
where we can all meet
and enjoy each other again -
and from then on,
always see the ordinary
as extraordinary
and truly blessed

Walking Into the New Year With Confidence

God Is With Us

(New Year celebrations had been restricted to a single household and the government was about to announce a new national lockdown.)

Now we have received the great Christmas gift of God himself coming to join us, we can face the New Year with confidence. He is born again in every family—good or not so good, loving or violent, united or broken, rich or poor. There are no outsiders. He is with us all and wants to be with us all, without preconditions. This is where we find our confidence here on earth and in eternity.

Because of this thing God has done, everything has changed beyond our wildest dreams. So now when parents gather on Judgement Day, the Lord will gently say, *'I was hungry and you fed me, thirsty and you gave me drink, naked and you clothed me, homeless and you sheltered me, imprisoned and you visited me. Come and enter the kingdom I have prepared for you.'*

And the parents will ask, *'Are you sure, Lord? When did we see you hungry and feed you?'* The Lord will reply, *'Do you not remember the way you carefully fed me when I was a baby, the way you loved me into my first little steps across the kitchen into your arms and later my bigger steps into the world? All the time that was me. Yes of course it was your child but it was me, your God, as well.'*

'When were you thirsty, Lord?' they will ask. *'I needed love and comfort; you took me onto your lap and I could hear your heart. I, your God, fell asleep in your arms, so secure and safe did I feel.'*

'But when were you naked and homeless, Lord?'

The Lord will reply: *'I was born naked and homeless and you sheltered me, first in your womb and then in your arms. In my rebellious years you stayed with me and forgave me over and over again. Whenever I came home, your face was always a smiling, warm welcome.'*

'But not in prison Lord, surely?'

The Lord will reply, *'There are many kinds of prison. When I was imprisoned in my fears at night, I cried out and you came and lifted me out into your arms. Years later, you lifted me from behind the bars of bigger fears—my own inadequacy, my intense emotions and the fears of my unknown life ahead. You were with me on every occasion. You gave me strength and confidence and set me free.'*

The Good News of Christmas is that what the Lord says to parents he says to all, because he has become flesh in each one of us. And he will point out to us where we have helped and supported him on our journey through life and in our daily interactions with people around us. We will probably be as surprised as those parents! But it is the Christmas message. It is the

Good News for all to hear. No matter where we find ourselves this New Year or in whatever circumstances, we are never alone. Our God is with us.

My wish for you this New Year is the same as for myself—that we hold on to the Christmas story right through this year. We have come through a difficult time together and I am confident it will only have strengthened our ties of love and affection as families and as a community. We pray for a New Year in which we can all meet and enjoy each other again. And from then on always see the ordinary as extraordinary and truly blessed.

The Baptism of the Lord

What a Swap Deal We Got!

The greatest swap of all time for the human race is the Baptism of Jesus. He takes our brokenness and sinfulness onto himself and in its place he gives us his glorious life of grace and goodness. It is as simple as that—a swap deal. This is what was going on when Jesus went into the River Jordan to be baptised by John the Baptist. As John poured the waters of the Jordan over Jesus, he was pouring all the sins of the world, of all generations past, present and future, including your sins and mine onto Jesus. Those muddied waters containing all the sins of the world, he took onto himself.

He carried those sins with him to Calvary. And when he was crucified, all our sins were crucified with him and were destroyed forever. When he rose on Easter Sunday, it was a victory over all sin and death. Now he instructed his disciples: *'Go and make disciples of all nations, baptising them in the name of the Father and of the Son and of the Holy Spirit. (Matthew 28:19).*

So when you and I were baptised, it was the crystal clean waters of God's life pouring onto us. And it is a process that is going on right through our lives. This is how our baptism and the baptism of Jesus are connected as one—two sides of the same coin. So there are two natures in each one of us, our own human nature and God's divine nature.

You will experience this in your own life at times: when you feel the pull to be a better person; when you feel guilty and unhappy with your behaviour; when you feel you have let yourself down because deep down you know you are a much better person; and in those moments when you feel a real desire to be more generous, more decent and more noble.

All of this—and much more that is going on in us—is Christ's baptism and our own baptism working itself out in our lives. It is fermenting and bringing to fruition a process of Christ becoming himself again in each one of us. This also throws a little light on the unrest we can experience from time to time. But what a swap and what a deal! That is why we say at Mass, '*This is the Lamb of God who takes away the sins of the world.*' We are all infinitely more fortunate than lottery winners!

So when you sit with the family around the table for your Sunday roast and Yorkshire puddings, raise a glass to this great feast day—the Baptism of Christ and yourself, grafted together forever.

Leaving Everything to Follow Him

'They left everything and followed him.' And so have you and I because this is our story too, not just once but ongoing, every day, unconsciously. The first step to realising this is to stop thinking of God as outside of us. He has left there and is now inside each one of us. Not only that, but he has also become us—that is what we mean by *'the Word was made flesh' (John 1:14)*. From the time we left the womb we have been on the move and constantly 'leaving everything and following him' without even being aware of it. It is a rhythm of life that goes on every day in your life and mine.

Think about it; you were a baby for a while but you left all of that and became a young girl or boy. Then you left that and became a teenager and then a young adult. You left that stage and moved on again to take on new challenges. Opportunities came your way and you moved off in another direction. You may have got married and brought up a family, or perhaps focused on your career, or become a full-time carer for someone. Here all the stages begin again for you. As a parent, you are being taken through all these stages again in your child. And in your career or in your role as a carer, you are always leaving where you are and moving on to what is coming next. You will leave today and move on to tomorrow and again to the next day. We are all in this drama. You and I are constantly leaving everything and following the Lord, just like the first disciples, without even being aware of it.

If we are not sure what the Lord is calling us to at this time in our lives, we only have to reflect on what preoccupied us last week and what was distracting us, what was keeping us awake and where we were finding joy and satisfaction. And because Christ not only lives in you, but has become you—in your preoccupations, your joys and your sorrows—so your concerns are his too.

Don't forget the things that happen outside of your control. Mark devotes the final quarter of his gospel to Jesus having things done to him that are outside his control. He is lovingly anointed but he is also abandoned and betrayed. He is arrested, a victim of denials. He is bound and handed over. He is scourged and crowned with thorns. He is helped to carry his cross but is also mocked. In the end, he is killed—a victim—and it is all so unfair.

This was all part of his life and it continues to be today. Now he is going on living his life in you and me and sometimes we experience some of this cruelty and injustice in our own lives or in the lives of our family and friends. But we are never alone. He is with us always and in the end we will discover to our great delight that he was the one who left everything to follow us.

Lessons Learned from My Atheist Friends

The more my atheist friends talk to me about the God they don't believe in, the more I find myself agreeing with them all the way. I don't believe in that God either. The real tragedy is how God has been presented in such a way, so for me, the most pressing need in our time is that as believing Christians we must have a clear and healthy notion of God. I say this because the God we worship is either making more disciples or more atheists, and it's as simple as that.

Our first task as believers is to rescue God from stupidity, narrowness, legality, rigidity, tribalism and everything else bad associated with God. Atheism and most anti-Church attitudes feed off bad religion. So we who believe and go to church should be examining ourselves more than defending ourselves. I say this with sympathy because all of us—priests and parishioners—will never do God justice.

What did Jesus reveal about God? he has no favourites—equality of nations, rich and poor, male and female, saint and sinner, good and bad—there are no outsiders, all are privileged. He had special compassion for the weak and the sinner, sitting with public sinners without first asking them to repent, offending the religious leaders by welcoming everyone and telling them God loves sinners and saints in the same way.

Jesus is critical of those who try to restrict access to him. He dies loving and forgiving those who are killing him. Jesus also makes clear that it is not necessarily those who profess God and religion who are his true followers, but those who do the will of God on earth. He makes clear that his message is Good News for the poor and that anything else is not his Gospel.

A Day Out with Our Heavenly Father

With our reflection this week we can sit down beside the writer of Psalm 8, who expresses our thoughts and feelings well.

Lord, when I see the heavens, the work of your hands
The moon and stars that you have arranged,
What are we that you should keep us in mind and care for us?
Yet you have made us little less than a God and put all these under our feet.

Now we are in lockdown and told to stay at home again, it is understandable that many are finding it difficult. So isn't it just as well we have a Heavenly Father who takes us out for a spin every day? I must confess I had not given this much thought until recently, but now I often find myself thinking of our daily trip. It is easy not to be aware of this space journey we are on with our Father because he gives us such a smooth ride that we can feel as though we are stationary and not on the move at all. Yet what a ride he takes us on. And now we have more time on our hands, I think it is well worth a reflection. Stay with me now and don't go away!

He has put us on board this planet earth that spins around its own axis at a speed of 1,000 miles per hour at the equator (600 miles per hour for us in the Boro). One circuit taking twenty-four hours gives us our days and nights. And because our Father can multitask, as we spin we are also on another circular journey as we orbit around the sun. Travelling at a speed of 66,000 miles per hour, this second journey takes 365 days to complete, giving us seasons. And so in all, we travel 595 million miles on our annual pilgrimage around the sun! But our Father isn't finished yet. As a member of a solar family composed of the sun and eight planets along with their moons, our earth is also racing outward into space at 43,000 miles per hour.

The cumulative effect of these three journeys is huge. In the space of one turnaround, we travel a million miles outward into space in a winding stairway-type path. So when you wake up in the morning and say you stayed at home last night and didn't go anywhere, you are only half right. You may have stayed at home, but you have ended up a million miles from where you were this time yesterday.

The point of our reflection is to awaken us to the reality of our earth's threefold movements now at this very moment. This awareness of distance, speed and order *must* give us a sense of awe and wonder. So, what more is there to say? With a Father who can guide all this, you and I are in very good and safe hands.

To qualify as members
of his Church
we must be sinners -
and know we are sinners

Ash Wednesday and its Ritual

In many ways we fall short and fail to live up to what we can be. On Ash Wednesday, the Church reminds us in a very striking way of this fact: '*Remember you are dust and to dust you will return,*' the priest says over each person and marks them with ashes. The whole community coming forward in this great general confession of failure and frailty is remembering we will die one day and we have made a mess of many things—and we confess this publicly.

In this ritual action, which stretches across the five continents, millions of people have made public that which we all know privately—that we are frail creatures, failures in what we really believe, and failing not least the very ones we love most. We fall short even of the standards we set ourselves.

On Ash Wednesday, the Church provides a kind of framework within which people can admit they are fallible, particularly in the business of living. When the priest looks at the rows of people coming up to receive the ashes it is, or it should be, one of life's most moving experiences. He hears them say in a ritual way that in the job of living, they have left much to be desired. And we all need to say just that to ourselves, to each other, and to God.

That is why we have Ash Wednesday. And although it is an admission of failure, nobody minds that you know it. The ritual has enabled us to say, 'I know I am inadequate; that's why I need your understanding, your forgiveness and your love.'

Of course, we will not be able to have our usual Ash Wednesday service in church this year, but what a glorious opportunity this is for us to perform our own personal ritual. Pick up a fistful of soil, look at it and feel its sacredness. As part of creation it transmits the Spirit of God to us. It produces our food, drink and medication, as well as sustaining our daily lives. We human beings are charged with the task of being stewards of it all. We could be doing a better job. A little prayer like, 'Father forgive us for we know not what we do' will be sufficient.

Snowdrops in the Cemetery

What is going on all around us?

I started walking through Linthorpe Cemetery during the first lockdown and I still pay a visit every now and then. What strikes me always is the great towering trees keeping vigil over the graves. Each one is like a devoted mother watching over her children as they sleep, some standing erect, others bending over as if tucking in their little ones. All are sheltering and protecting in the way only mothers know. There is always a serenity and peace surrounding the place—the kind you find only in a cemetery. But it has another peace too, of a very different kind—that quiet tranquillity you see in the bond between a mother and her child. This place seems to hold both, and they belong together. At a glance, every grave is a cradle, each comfortably bedding a loved one and all have an adoring mother watching over with such loving protection.

Just now the place is taken over with the quiet hush of snowdrops. They seem to be gathering everywhere, forming groups in little clusters, whispering something, and the rumour is spreading. There are more and more appearing, so small and fragile and their language is silent; they can say more that way. It seems all the really important things are said in silence. But what are the snowdrops saying? Could it be that all these ones have risen from their sleep? Are they announcing that every grave is now an empty tomb and they have all risen with their Lord and just like him, have gone ahead into Galilee?

Galilee was the place where Jesus and his followers shared so many treasured memories and precious moments. It was where they first got to know each other and where Jesus would tell Mary Magdalene they should meet him on that first Easter morning. In the same way, all these ones are alive with him now and are to be found by their loved ones in their Galilee—those places where precious memories are shared, where they blossom into their real selves and bring life and laughter to all around. These are the places where their families and friends will be meeting them now.

Every time I come away from Linthorpe Cemetery, those snowdrops remain with me—or do they? Could I have met the lovely gentle and fragile Mary Magdalene announcing that the Lord has risen, and so have all who were buried there? Maybe Mary Magdalene accompanies me home every time I leave that place and I do not realise it? Or am I just talking to myself again?

Reflecting on Abraham

Human Sacrifice

We read in our bibles the account of how Abraham took Isaac, the lovely son he and Sarah had been waiting so long for, to sacrifice to God. What is it about? Well firstly we have to remember that our ancestors were growing all the time in their vision of God. Let us resist the temptation to look back on the story from where we are and from our standpoint now. Not that it's much better, but the point I want to make is they were projecting themselves on to God with the result that the God they believed in was harsh, a monster that had to be placated. And so when Abraham was going off up the hill with his son and his load of wood for the sacrifice, he was one of so many more Abrahams who were living in that culture. It was a culture of human sacrifice and Abraham was going up there in that context. And then as he is about to offer the sacrifice, he can hear God deep down inside himself saying, *'Look, stop ... stop, Abraham! That is not what I want. That is not who I am. No, no, no! Do not sacrifice a human being. I do not and have not ever wanted that.'*

Abraham, because of his faith, was the first who could see through the fog of the culture he was living in and he became aware that God is not as the people had understood him. How much we need an Abraham in our culture! How much we need an Abraham in every country to lead us and to show us out of our culture. Because human sacrifice was not only something that took place with our ancestors. Tragically, human sacrifice is going on all the time. So many countries still have the death penalty. It only took the pandemic to open up to us the state of our care homes. Those wonderful people who have been looking after all our elderly people, doing heroic work—and the virus exposed how little they have been supported by our government and by us as a people, as a culture. The number of people who died in our care homes compared with the rest of our society was both shocking and frightening. Human sacrifice among our elderly is real and we need an Abraham to open up our governments, our leaders and ourselves to take our elderly more seriously and to care for them.

Jo Whiley is in the news. She is a BBC DJ who was shocked, upset and horrified that she would be invited to have the vaccine before her sister, Frances, who has learning difficulties. Human sacrifice can be seen in the way we care. Could we care better for people with learning disabilities or other difficulties?

Need we speak about war and the human sacrifice it brings? It is sad to say that Great Britain is second only to the United States in the number of military weapons we export every year. In 2018, according to official figures, we exported more than £14bn worth. Sixty per cent arrived at their destination in the Middle East. We see on our televisions those who are on the receiving end of those weapons.

Human sacrifice is all around us. But we have other names for it. We sanitise it and call it something like 'collateral damage' because it doesn't sound as bad. If we have to see it on our televisions, we get a warning from the newsreader saying, *'Some of our viewers might find this next item upsetting...'* We are all caught up in a fog where we don't see what is going on all around us. Because it is our government, speaking in our name, getting the huge profits from it and I am benefitting, and you are benefitting. We all benefit from the profits of those weapons.

And then, of course, there is the increasing demand for abortion. A culture can make everything possible and can make anything happen. This is not a time for blaming but it is a time for observing—and seeing that we live in a culture of human sacrifice.

So Abraham, come into our lives. You are our father in faith. Show us the way, as our God says. *'No, no, no... I don't want any more of this.'*

Our First Holy Communion

The purpose of this reflection is not to make us more knowledgeable—God knows we have our bellyful of that already. It is more an attempt to digest some of the knowledge we already have and give us a sense of awe and wonder of the world around us. But it is especially to make us more aware of how totally dependent we are on all of creation and our planet earth. We are living in a big communion of sun, earth and rain (another blessed trinity) and we are constantly blessed by all three. Yes, indeed we are walking on holy ground.

Pope Francis, with the aid of modern science, is teaching us that another holy communion began a long time ago and is ongoing. And although there is something marvellous going on around us, Francis is concerned because we know more about the universe than any previous generation and yet we have less intimacy with it. It has lost its mystical wonder for us and does not expand our appreciation. It has not enhanced how we treat each other and how we treat the earth, nor has it impacted on how we relate to God. The reason for this, Francis laments, is because our universe story has remained at a scientific level. We need a spirituality that opens us to our new-found knowledge about the world and how it is charged with the Spirit of God.

Let us reflect on the food we eat. Bread comes from wheat and that wheat gets its energy from the sun, which is ninety-three million miles away from us. The light and warmth of the sun takes about eight minutes to reach the earth. This light and warmth, combined with the rain, falls on the seed and it puts down roots to anchor it in the soil. Nourished by this combination the seed develops a stem, leaves and a head to produce the wheat. Now your slice of toast you are enjoying for breakfast is the result of this communion between sun, earth and rain. So we can see that eating is a real communion event, where we are connecting with the whole of creation.

Not only that but think of the labour involved in the 'work of human hands'. From harvesting to getting the bread on the table, there are people working together—another communion. The very act of eating together transforms us. This new energy is flowing through us now and we are energising each other. The sun is the source of all this, together with the rain. The earth is the recipient and we are the benefactors. 'Mother Earth'—mother of all mothers—gives us 'our daily bread'. And here is our God coming to meet us in it all. '*Take this all of you and eat.*'

So we understand that our universe is a womb and here we are, in it, part of it and totally dependent on it until we are born into the fullness of life. But for now we belong here, and our connection to the earth is vital. We must reverence this communion at all times. Now we are beginning to recognise that our universe is much more sacred than we had been aware and that our Holy Communion at Mass stretches much further than we had realised. The hope of Pope Francis is that our sense of wonder in both—the universe and the Mass—will grow more and more.

A Love Letter to the Institutional Church

(Coming up to first anniversary of the initial lockdown)

Two comments frequently expressed over the last year are, 'I really miss the Church' and 'I am managing fine without it.' I suspect both express part of each one of us because the Church is part of who we are and yet we are all so different.

This Church is sinless because of Christ. And at the same time it is sinful and scandalous because of us. So it is understandable when some of us say, 'I can manage fine with Christ. It is this frustrating Church I can't be bothered with.' The problem with this is that I will end up with a Christ of my own making and not the Christ of the gospels. He gathered all kinds of characters and was associated with so many undesirable people that he got a bad reputation. He lived, worked, socialised and died with these people. And in our days of social distancing, it is worth noting that his closest companions at the end were two thieves who died with him. Even those two were a mixed bunch!

Carlo Carretto was an Italian monk who spent many years living in the Sahara Desert with the Bedouin people. His was a life of prayer and he wrote many books to help us know God better. He loved God and the Church and so when he is criticising, it is very much as an insider—and with love. But a few years before he died in 1988, he wrote a book about his struggles with God and the Church. He ends the book with a love letter addressed to the visible institutional Church. I paraphrase it here:

'How much I must criticise you, my Church, and yet how much I love you! You have made me suffer more than anyone and yet I owe you more than I owe anyone. I should like to see you destroyed and yet I need your presence. You have given me much scandal and yet you alone have made me understand holiness. Never in the world have I seen anything more compromised, more false. Yet never have I touched anything more pure, more generous or more beautiful. Countless times I have felt like slamming the door of my soul in your face—and yet every night I have prayed that I might die in your sure arms! No, I cannot be free of you, for I am one with you, even if not completely you. And where should I go? Is it to build another Church? But I cannot build another Church without the same defects, for they are my own defects. And again, if I were to build another Church it would be my Church, not Christ's Church. No, I am old enough. I know better!'[1]

We are the Church chosen by Christ to be his body in the world, made up from first to last only of sinners. To qualify as members of his Church, we must be sinners—and know we are sinners. He chose Peter, who betrayed him, as our first leader to keep us all humble, as he is the best we've got. Now the Holy Spirit sees us all as immaculate and beautiful under the guise of sinners. He continues to re-establish our spotless souls, no matter how many times we fall. This is our Church.

---

1. Carretto C, 2000, *I Sought and I Found, My Experience of God and of the Church,* Orbis Books, USA

Setting the Scene for Holy Week

Leading up to the Champions League coverage during the week (football, for the uninitiated), to set the scene and get us ready for the match, we were taken back to previous games the two teams had played. Then the commentator broke in and said, *'Now after this short break we'll be back with the real game—and it is live.'*

I thought to myself, that's exactly what we do in Holy Week. We play back over past events of Christ's life, his Passion, Death and Resurrection, in order to get us ready and alert for where it is taking place now. Then as the commentator said, *'We'll be back with the game—and it is live.'* So as we leave the Church, we are going out into Christ's Passion, death and Resurrection now, where it is live. And because he has become flesh in us, he is going through this again now in each one of us at different times and stages of our lives.

He is constantly before our eyes. We see him drowning in the Mediterranean over and over again as dinghy boats sink, or when he is successful in crossing, he is refused asylum. And when he could not escape, we have seen him tortured, murdered or buried under piles of rubble and in mass graves. We see him all around us and on our TV screens and in our newspapers, still suffering, rejected, despised and humiliated before our eyes. He is everywhere to be seen in his Passion and death.

But we can see evidence of his Resurrection, too. And this is his great victory and triumph because he is rising up in and through all this death and destruction. There are thousands of people reaching out with food, clothes, medicine, money and whatever else is needed. So as we look ahead to Holy Week, we remind ourselves that Passion, death and Resurrection are one. Resurrection will have the last word as death and destruction are swallowed up in victory.

Palm Sunday

This Palm Sunday Gospel shows you the fickleness of the crowd, doesn't it? There they are this Sunday, all welcoming Jesus and before next Sunday they will be shouting, *'Crucify him!'* So the moral of the story is to never follow the crowd. Every football manager knows the fickleness of the crowd, doesn't he?

Looking ahead to next weekend, the celebrations have become so complicated that most of us don't understand a word of what goes on. Everyone is uptight and thinking, 'Can we get through the service?' So let's keep it simple. Saturday, just like Thursday and Friday is like a three-act play.

Act One on Saturday is outside the Church. It's the ceremony of light and there's a bonfire.

Now, centuries ago, the whole thing would have had an atmosphere of a barbecue and the crowd would have been celebrating. They would be in no hurry to leave and it would have been in the context of that celebration that the fire would have been lit. The fire is celebrating that Christ is risen among us and from that fire, a candle is lit. It's called the Paschal or Easter Candle and as it is brought into Church, the crowd all walk behind it as a symbol and a sign of the Risen Christ walking into the church and us following him.

Once we're inside and when everybody is gathered, we sing to that Paschal Candle that symbolises Christ, and then it is brought through the church congregation. It is like when a hero is shouldered and brought through a crowd and the crowd rejoice and celebrate, the difference being if a hero is brought through it's about the hero but with Christ's Resurrection, he's not a Lone Ranger; it's not a one-man show. No! You and I and all creation, past generations and future generations all rose with him and are all continuing to rise with him at death. The Paschal Candle going around the church congregation is celebrating all of us. It's our story! It's our life! We are all risen to a new life and that is what the first act is about.

Act Two is the act of water. The candle is taken and plunged into the water to make it holy water—or Easter water. In that water, all people for the coming year will be baptised and that baptism is Jesus' pledge: *'Look, my eternal life is in you! You will live forever.'* The priest sprinkles the people with the water as a sign of Christ's new life within us. That is what we celebrate with the water and that's it for Act Two. Keep it as simple as can be.

Act Three is the readings, which are simply about looking back at the way our God has been dealing with our ancestors and with us down through the generations, and his faithfulness to us even though our ancestors—and us in our turn—have been unfaithful again and again because we are not able to keep to our commitments. But our God continues loving us like a mother loving her children and he understands our weakness.

There are seven Old Testament readings and with the passing of centuries this celebration has become just a religious ceremony, disconnected from our lives, and that's why we get confused and uninterested in it. We don't understand it —priests and people—and that's the shame of it, because the whole thing is about our lives. The purpose of each reading is not to give us more information. No! It's like putting a spotlight on us. It's like saying: *'Have you seen? Have you noticed? Can you see better? Do you understand now? Can you see clearly?'*

So I'll take just three readings from the Old Testament and say a word on them quickly. Creation: When creation is being read, it's not about listening to that account. It is saying, *'Look and see where God is creating now. Look at all the new life—animals, birds, children, fish. Every place you look—trees, fruit, crops. Wherever you go, there is new life growing. Can you see God creating?'* That's what creation is about, shining a light on us so that we can live more and with more life. That's the first reading.

The second is from the Book of Exodus. God is bringing our ancestors out of slavery in Egypt and into the Promised Land. You know, that's not just about listening to what happened long ago. I can just reflect on my own life and what God has brought me through, as far back as I can remember, and what he still keeps bringing me through, what he brought all of us through and keeps bringing us through, what he brought our families through and what he keeps bringing them through. Look at the way all that is going on. Be aware of it. That's what this reading is about. Take another one then, the prophet. *'Come to the waters all you who are thirsty, though you have no money come... buy corn at no price, everything free.' (Isaiah 55:1)* It is not about reflecting on that but rather the things that I have that are free: my life, my health, my family, my children, my grandchildren, my parents, my grandparents, my friends. All the things we cherish, all the things we couldn't live without, the people who delight in us and those who give us friendship. All of these are free gifts. That's the point of the readings.

So that's just a quick reflection on Easter Saturday and what it's about. It is to celebrate our life and all that's going on in it.

'What good is it
Christ rising from the grave
if he does not rise in me?'

(Karl Rahner)

Easter and Eucharist

Christ is raised to new life. He took us all with him through that three-day journey and we now share this new resurrected life with him. It is not just a victory for Christ; it is our victory, too. Because of Easter we can understand the Mass better and also know what God expects from us after feasting at his Eucharistic banquet.

We have heard the expression, 'There is no such thing as a free lunch.' This is true of the Eucharist more than we realise. There are strings attached. The Feeding of the Five Thousand is still going on. Jesus gave the food to the disciples to distribute among the multitude. You and I are those disciples today. At Mass, Jesus is food for you. Now you are food for the multitude.

We cannot just come and receive Eucharist then keep it for ourselves. *'You received without charge, give without charge' (Matthew 10:8). 'To whom much is given, much will be expected' (Luke 12:48).*

The Easter Christ is saying to all of us, *'I am not in the world any longer in human form but you are in the world. And I believe in you and will be watching over you to provide help when you need it. You are my hands. You are my feet. You are my voice. You are my heart. In fact, you are me, because I have become you. You are my disciple.'*

What a privilege! This is Easter and Eucharist for Easter People!

The Blessings of Easter to you and all in your care.

The Mass is Ended—Go in Peace

At the end of Mass we are sent out with the words, '*The Mass is ended. Go in peace.*' This does not mean the Mass is now over and you can go home. God is not saying, '*You can go now and thanks for coming!*'

He is saying: '*I have invited you to my banquet. I have nourished you with Eucharist and my Word. I am so involved with you that the way I am in the world from now on is through you and also through the many people who do not know me and yet allow me to have my way in them. I want to continue being light to the world, leaven in the dough, salt of the earth and I need your help to do that.*

'*The only way I can get to the people you meet this week will be through you. If you can let me take your place this week, just imagine how I will be with those people. Watch the way I will speak and listen to them, see how I take delight in each one and notice the trail of life and joy that follows me.*

'This opportunity is yours every week and all of this is called "ordinary life". This is why I need you to allow me to have my way in you. It is what I mean when I send you out from Mass with the words, "The Mass is ended. Go in peace". If you don't understand why I invite you to my banquet every week, then you will never understand why and how I am sending you out.'

Go in peace.

Talking to Myself this Easter

What Are We Celebrating?

The Resurrected Life of Christ is flowing through all of creation, giving us bud and blossom, crops and food of all kinds. Our task as human beings is to cooperate with Christ in the same way as the rest of nature and let the gifts of the Spirit flow through us to give life and nourish those around us.

Karl Rahner, a leading Catholic theologian and a saintly man, wrote: '*What good is it Christ rising from the grave if he does not rise in me?*' What did he mean by this? he was saying the Resurrection of Christ is not something to waste words on—what I believe or don't, indeed how I understand or don't understand it. His followers were confused and their faith shattered but they were changed. Slowly, they came to realise Christ did not rise alone; they had been involved in it, too. They had all risen to a new state and they could feel it within. For the most part, they went along with that flow of new life and yet at times they fell back to old ways. You and I were with him, too, as were all past and future generations. Now don't go away; stay with me!

The challenge for you and me is not just to believe Jesus rose from the grave but more importantly, to believe that regardless of our mistakes, wounds, sins and hurts, we can begin each day fresh and new and clean again. Regardless of what we've done or failed to do, our future is always full of new possibilities. Resurrection is much more than something that comes some time after death. It is also about daily rising from the many mini graves within which we so often find ourselves.

How does belief in the Resurrection help us rise from these mini graves? By keeping us open to surprise, newness and freshness in our lives. Not an easy thing to do. We are human and we cannot avoid falling into depression, bitterness, sin, cynicism and the tiredness that comes to all of us, young or old. We too have our crucifixions like Jesus. More than one grave awaits us and we've been through a few already. Our faith in the Resurrection invites us not just to live beyond these but to live again and again and again!

Yes, little Good Fridays come to all of us. It is the rhythm of life. Everywhere we look now, we can see that all of nature itself is rising from the grave and growth and new life is appearing in all its forms. We are part of all this. We can see new life everywhere and feel it within ourselves. We know now, deep inside there is a life that has been bringing us out of our small graves and will continue over and over before that life raises us from our final grave. Death and Resurrection are two aspects of a single event.

Faith in the Resurrection is much more than a creed we recite in church. Parrots could do that. It is new life flowing through the whole of nature, ourselves included. And we human beings experience it as love, joy, peace, patience, kindness, fortitude, resilience, goodness, gratitude and delight. The measure of our belief in the Resurrection is in the flow of these qualities from us. And the judges are those around us every day. They are at the receiving end of all this lovely flow of life.

'By their fruits you will know them' (Matthew 7:16). Indeed, 'What good is it Christ rising from the grave if he does not rise in me?'

Vocations Sunday

I can think of nothing better on Vocations Sunday than to send you a reflective poem. This poem makes me think of all you great people who are living your vocation to the full as mothers and fathers, grandmothers and grandfathers, aunts and uncles, brothers and sisters, cousins and friends—whoever and whatever you are, because your very life is your vocation.

There is an African saying, 'It takes a whole village to raise a child' and I know the same is true for us here. It takes a whole community, not just a parent to raise a child. We all have an important role to play in bringing up our children so that they too can live their lives to the full.

A Noble Boy

The woman was old and feeble and grey,
And bent with the chill of the winter's day,
The street was wet with recent snow,
And the woman's feet were weary and slow,
She stood at the crossing and waited long,
Alone, uncared for, amid the throng,
Down the street with laughter and shout,
Glad in the freedom of 'school let out'
Came the boys, like a flock of sheep,
Hailing the snow, piled white and deep.
Past the woman, so old and grey,
Hastened the children on their way,
Nor offered a helping hand to her,
So meek, so timid, afraid to stir.

At last came one of the merry troop
The kindest boy of all the group;
He paused beside her and whispered low,
'I'll help you across if you wish to go.'
He guided the trembling feet along,
Proud that his own were firm and strong,
Then back again to his friends he went,
His young heart happy and well content,
'She is somebody's mother boys you know,
Although she is old and poor and slow,
And I hope some fellow will lend a hand,

To help my mother—you understand
If e'er she be poor and old and grey,
When her own dear boy is far away.'

And 'somebody's mother' bowed low her head,
In her home that night and the prayer she said,
Was, 'God be kind to the noble boy,
Who is somebody's son and pride and joy.'

Mary Dow Brine (1878)

Blessing

What are we doing when we bless? People come to me from time to time and request that I bless something for them. I am not sure what goes on in us when we do this for we cannot express it fully nor do we need to. There are some things in life that cannot be captured or contained in words.

My mother blessed us with holy water before we went to school every day. My father blessed the crops with holy water before planting and did the same to the cows in the springtime before they were put out in the fields after the winter lock-in. At our Easter Vigil I blessed water in the church for baptisms. So what is a blessing? And what do we do when we bless? We find the answer in the first pages of the Bible.

In the story of creation, at the end of each day God looked on what he had done and '*saw that it was good.*' On the sixth day, when God created the man and the woman and completed creation, it is even more emphasised. God looked and saw what he had done 'and *indeed it was very good' (Genesis 1:31).* God is still looking at his creation and saying, *'It is indeed very good.'*

We see a similar blessing at the baptism of Jesus. The heavens open and God's voice is heard to say, *'This is my beloved son in whom I am well pleased' (Matthew 3:17).* Jesus wants us to look at our own lives and see ourselves as always blessed, no matter how difficult our situation may be. Blessed are you when you are poor, when you mourn, when you are hungry and thirsty, when people hate you and abuse you and persecute you *(Matthew Chapter 5).* In all those situations, Jesus was blessed and he was loved and he knew it. He wants you and me to know it too because we are blessed and loved by our Heavenly Father.

Parents and grandparents are constantly blessing their little ones, perhaps without even knowing it and it doesn't have to be in words. It can be in a glance of pride and delight, an urge to care and protect. These blessings are flowing constantly in family life and it is in the shadow of these blessings that children grow into confident young people. Gradually, we begin to realise we are the ones who are blessed by what we bless. Parents and grandparents know only too well how much they are blessed by their children and grandchildren.

And what is going on when we are blessing water in the church for baptisms? Just like the families realising how they are blessed by their children, so we too are realising how we are blessed by water. It quenches our thirst, gives us a refreshing cup of tea and flows from the tap so we can wash up or take an invigorating shower or a warm, relaxing bath. It comes from the skies to water the earth, flowers, plants and crops. It comes to our aid so many times every day. Just as God takes delight in his creation, we do the same, delighting in our children, water, crops, animals, the whole of creation. A blessing is saying, *'Thank you, thank you, thank you,'* and the Eucharist is the Big Thank You.

Saying Goodbye to My Last Daffodil

Is the daffodil with its short visit trying to tell us something about the brevity of our lives and so to treasure every moment with our loved ones? The angel came to Mary with a message from God and the angel left her. The daffodil came to us and the daffodil left us.

Saying goodbye to the last daffodil in my garden this week, I realised how I have enjoyed them this year more than ever. They would bob their little heads as if endlessly looking for attention. And that would bring me out of the house to join them and at the same time, out of myself—my mind, my plans and various bondages that hold my attention. I would be released from myself and set free for a little while, living in delightful freedom.

The daffodils were like clusters of excited little children all trying to speak together and they seemed to be saying:

'Can you see us? Here we are surrounded by our friends, so many of us and we have just arrived. We get bigger and brighter every day. We are so surprised at our capacity to change and to open out in new ways. Our surroundings are changing all the time and that shows off different aspects of our beauty. At times the wind is calm and gentle; other times it is strong and gusty and we love to dance in tune with its various moods. Sometimes the sun comes out and then fades away just as quickly. That gives us different shades and colours. It can be like a fashion show at these times as we change from one moment to the next.

'The clouds are our real delight when they wander over us playing hide and seek with the sun, especially when they bring the rain. And how lovely that is to feel the soft life-giving drops touch and caress our petals with such care and tenderness. Then the water trickles gently down our stem, through our bed of soil and right into our roots. It gives us such new vitality that we feel like jumping up and down or even flying like the birds, but that is not our nature. So we sway and flutter together and abandon ourselves to the wind as we dance. Oh, how it delights us when people notice, when they stop and look at us closely to see how lovely we are. At such moments we feel beautiful and rather humble too.

'Do you think people could come more often just to see us or do they only have eyes for what is "useful"? A daffodil isn't "useful" we know that—except when they cut away a few of our number to beautify their homes. Is there something wrong with being gentle, vulnerable and beautiful, living in harmony with everyone and everything? Because that is all we do and yet we seem to be ignored, though not by everybody of course. Some folk will stand and be quiet with us—usually the older folk and the little children. And yet, it seems to take some people longer to get in tune with the whole of creation than it takes us daffodils. Could that be the reason people have to stay longer on this earth?

Do they have a lot of lessons still to learn? We don't know, and that's why we would like to spend a lot more time together with people.'

The next day, my last daffodil had bowed its little head and given up its spirit.

Spending Time in God's Company

The whole of the gospel this Sunday is Jesus speaking to his Father and praying for his disciples. It reminds us of the importance of taking time out of our busy lives to spend time with God, to pray and to rest in his company.

I read a lovely commentary on this by the scripture scholar William Barclay. He said we cannot work unless we get enough sleep and we cannot sleep unless we tire ourselves out with activity. In the same way, if we are too busy to spend time with God, we cannot experience the rest only he can give.

Of course the time we spend with God is not an alternative to spending time with people. *'I am not asking you to remove them from the world...'* *(John 17:15)*. On the contrary, we meet God in a quiet, restful place and then we meet—and serve—him in the people we encounter every day, *'As you sent me into the world, I have sent them into the world ...' (John 17:18)* because prayer without action is not real prayer.

These are not two different sections of our lives. They are two prongs of the same fork and they work together, just as our heart and lungs do. Our God offers to everyone, free of charge, life in abundance and if we spend a little time in his restful company each day and recognise and serve him in the people we meet, then we can discover for ourselves this wonderful gift.

I'd like to say to the Holy Spirit
'Tell me,
what you have got going on
in the world these days?'

Pentecost

What is the Holy Spirit Doing in the World Today?

We all know that feeling when we meet someone and they ask, '*What have you got on today?*' and we don't quite know what to say. I know I often find it difficult to answer because I don't always know what I have on. Well over the past few days, as Pentecost was coming up, I'd thought I'd like to ask the Holy Spirit, '*What have you got on today, Holy Spirit? I don't want you to talk to me about creation and about people all over the world. I can see you beautifully there, everywhere around* me. *But tell me what you have got on in the world these days?*'

I have been researching a few facts, and the interesting thing I seemed to be hearing from the Holy Spirit is the huge growth and shift in location in the Catholic population throughout the world.

In 1910, sixty-five per cent of all Catholics in the world lived in Europe. Today, Europe accounts for less than twenty-four per cent of all Catholics. Over time, there has been a huge explosion of faith in what we call the 'global south'. For example, seventy per cent of all Catholics in the world now live in the southern hemisphere. The Philippines has become the third-largest national Catholic population. At the same time, there has been a huge expansion in South America, Brazil, Argentina, Central America and Mexico. Those places are exploding with people coming into the Church.

In 1900, there were two million Catholics throughout the whole of Africa. In 2020, there were 240 million, and today there are 256 million. That's sixteen million more Catholics than there were in 2020! The Democratic Republic of the Congo, for example, has a population of more than 110 million and is estimated to have 35 million Catholics—about a third of the total population.

Another interesting fact I learned is that there are more Christians of various denominations attending church every Sunday in China than in the whole of Europe. So I am beginning to see what the Holy Spirit is up to today! The way the Church is growing and exploding is a very different story from the one we hear in the media.

In the west, churches are emptying and I often wonder if the Holy Spirit is trying to say to us: *'Work with me like the people of the southern hemisphere, a Church of the people and run by the people, helped, guided and supported by the clergy, not the other way round!'* It seems the Church is exploding where it is being treated as Christ was treated, where it is being persecuted and is suffering and has all kinds of calumny spoken against it. There we find it alive and vibrant, filled with the gifts of the Spirit.

Our Church in the west, by contrast, is like a potted plant whose roots have no room to grow and so end up strangling the very plant itself. Here, in some areas we have a very hierarchical Church that tends to be fixated with issues of dogma and tradition. And we can see for ourselves the pain and torment they are continually bringing to Pope Francis on issues of tradition rather than on life and vitality and the mission of the Church.

The Holy Spirit is ahead of us and has seen this clearly and so for the first time in the Church's history, has given us a pope from south of the equator. It is understandable then that this pope comes with a very different agenda from his predecessors. Francis invites us to listen to and not lecture those on the periphery and to reach out to the poor and marginalised. Here is where we will find the Holy Spirit, he tells us. We are finding this difficult in our western Church because we have been used to lecturing from the centre. Listening is a new experience both for ourselves, and for our hierarchy.

I will finish off with just another little thought. I worked in Africa for a few years. It struck me that the seminaries were bursting at the seams with crowds of young men training for the priesthood and yet the ratio of priests to people continued to fall because the number of people flocking into the Church was infinitely greater than the thousands of young men joining the seminaries.

The answer to our shortage of priests in the west is not to turn to Africa. With the best will in the world, that may only end up masking what the Spirit is trying to tell us. If we know and understand anything at all about these places and the number of Catholics there, we will realise they are far worse off for priests than we are. So how dare we ask Africa, Asia or South America, or any of these places to send us priests? Those priests have more than enough to do in their own countries.

In the meantime, it is good news to know, at a time when our churches are emptying in Europe, that on a global level the Church is full, vibrant and growing as never before and with more people going to Sunday Mass and receiving the sacraments than at any time since the apostles climbed down from the upper room. It is guided by the Holy Spirit and we belong to that Church.

Trinity in You and Trinity in God

Trinity is as much in you and me as it is in God and it is not a puzzle to be solved; it is a story to be told.

There is a deep, silent place in you and me. It might be called the unconscious, the soul, God, personality. Call it what you like, what is important is that it is in you and me and out of that place you and I come to meet the world each day. However, we may not always come out as the same person. We use phrases like, 'He got out of the wrong side of the bed', 'I was beside myself last Tuesday' and 'I was trying to catch up with myself yesterday.' All this is Trinity language, suggesting every one of us is more than one person—and yet there is only the one me!

This silent place in us deserves a little attention. More than ninety-nine per cent of the universe is silent and you and I, being children of the universe, are made ninety-nine per cent silent, too—even if we are gabby.

We need to visit that place frequently and spend a little time with ourselves. If we go through life without having times of silence, we may never really get to know ourselves. So visit yourself regularly. Take yourself aside for a chat. This might sound foreign to many of us as our churches, workplaces and schools are not equipped to introduce us to silence—so much so that you might be feeling a little uneasy now and thinking I am getting a little too deep. Don't worry, I will just make one more point and then I'll stop.

Caring for our mental health is an issue very much with us. Depression is all too common in our society and it is not surprising when we break down under the pressures of life. Yet even the experience of mental ill-health can give an insight into the mystery of the Trinity because it is when we are not functioning well that we can take time to observe, pause, reflect and be amazed.

Trinity can draw our attention to this miracle beyond understanding that is at work in us every day. This *is* Trinity.

Eucharist as Homecoming

I must thank Cardinal Timothy Radcliffe for inspiring this reflection. I was reading about his experience of celebrating the Eucharist in Rwanda and it prompted me to share one of my own experiences. It's just one more straw from the haystack of the mystery of the Eucharist to reflect on. Put your own experience into it; only then will it make sense. When was the last time you came to church troubled? Did you find rest? How or with whom?

During my time in Kenya, I found myself in a refugee camp where families were living under plastic sheets. Innocent people, cleared out of their homes and land because warring tribes and government officials were fighting their battles and of course it is always the people who pay the price. They have a saying: *'When elephants fight, it is the grass that suffers.'* Celebrating Eucharist in situations like this, the most eloquent preacher is lost for words but is with the people in their suffering. Here we are at the very heart of Eucharist. It catches up everything that is going on in our lives; all is embraced and held in this simple action and command: *'Do this in memory of me.'*

This may strike you as a very painful situation and it is, but no less painful than the average gathering at our Eucharist every week, though that is not as visible because most of those crosses are internal and as a result are carried alone. But people are coming into our church with their heavy burdens, hoping to find a homecoming and 'rest for their souls'.

As we become aware of this, we realise more and more that good liturgy needs to be prepared, yet in the end it is the responsibility of the whole congregation. *'Be alert, stay awake' (Mark 13:33).* We receive Eucharist in order to pass it on to those around, beginning in church. If we are to experience Eucharist as a homecoming when we are overburdened, if Christ is to reach out and welcome us, he will need everyone to co-operate. Then all will feel accepted and included no matter what we have done or failed to do. He gave us the Eucharist on the night before he died to let us know he is with us always—in life, in suffering, in death and beyond. We are in safe hands.

Feast of the Sacred Heart

Many of our doctrines and devotions have been so frozen over for centuries that they are no longer recognisable. They are rich and life-giving, full of spiritual nourishment but sadly they have not been passed down, opened up and explained in such a way that we can locate them in our lives and experience. They have been placed in cold storage and we are all the poorer for that. Devotion to the Sacred Heart is just one of them.

Last Friday we celebrated the feast of the Sacred Heart, a popular devotion in Catholic communities. We have churches, parishes and schools dedicated to the Sacred Heart. The origin of this devotion began in the seventeenth century when a nun in France claimed to have seen apparitions of Christ. Sadly, like so many doctrines and devotions in our Church, this one has never evolved or grown in a way that makes sense to us in our lives. Its whole message and symbolism has been fossilised and is now imprisoned in sentimentality. The focus is taken away from the stuff of our lives and transferred into statues and pictures with lighted candles. As a result, it doesn't make any real demand on us or challenge our way of life. We can easily light a candle before the statue, say a few prayers and walk away calling it 'devotion to the Sacred Heart'. Nothing could be further from the truth. Christ wants much more from you and me than lighting candles before his statue.

We can catch a glimpse of what real devotion means when we look at a picture of the Sacred Heart and read its symbolism. The heart is surrounded with a crown of thorns and on top of the heart is a cross. The message is clear: this devotion is not for the faint-hearted, but for full-blooded and burning hearts. There is nothing sentimental about this devotion. Christ is saying to us, 'Can you be baptised with the baptism with which I was baptised? Can I live in you? Can my (sacred) heart beat inside your ribcage today? This is the devotion I want. Can I trust you? And if you say yes (as my mother did), you may well experience, as she did, a crown of thorns and the cross. Do not be scandalised by this.'

'If they persecuted me they will persecute you too' (John 15:20). But what I will promise is *'life in abundance' (John 10:10)* and *'I am with you always' (Matthew 28:20).*

Sacred Heart people are easily recognisable, even though many of them will not have heard of the Sacred Heart. They are the ones who give of themselves. They put their whole heart into what they do and who they are. They live for their children, partner, friends, neighbours and work colleagues. They are life-givers and we are drawn towards them. We come away from their company refreshed and renewed and we look forward to meeting them again. They are to be found in every walk of life and they come in every type of personality. They can be social and noisy or quiet and reserved but they are themselves, and we are enriched by their presence because they give us new life.

True devotion to the Sacred Heart is the realisation that all our lives are sacred. Every heart is a sacred heart: *'What you do to one of these you do to me' (Matthew 25:40).* Every experience we have in life is an ongoing conversation between Christ and ourselves—one sacred heart to another! And the point of lighting a candle and saying a prayer at the statue is to enable us to become more aware of this great mystery.

(The government had planned to end all Covid-19 restrictions by June 21st, but due to rising cases of the Delta variant this was delayed. Most restrictions were finally lifted on July 19th 2021)

Afterword

The days we have been reliving in these pages may now be fading memories. It's hard to believe we were really unable to visit each other, meet our friends at work or even worship together in our parishes. Life has returned to 'normal'—although for so many who lost loved ones, it will never be the same. Yet, in those dark days, we discovered something new about Christ's enduring presence, and how his love surrounds us always, especially in times of trial and separation.

Let us not forget the lessons solitude brought: the quiet power of faith, the yearning for communion with each other and our shared communion with our God and the love that is there even when we are forced to be apart. May we carry this awareness as we move forward together in faith and hope, ever mindful that Christ remains with us in every moment, drawing us closer to one another and to him.

Tom O'Neill

McGeary Media

Printed in Dunstable, United Kingdom

73059064R00117